Strings and Hide

Olga Fernández

Strings and Hide

EDITORIAL

José Martí

EDITORIAL JOSÉ MARTÍ
Publicaciones en Lenguas Extranjeras

Original Title in Spanish: *A pura guitarra y tambor*
Translation: *Esther Mosak and Margarita Zimmerman*
Editing: *Iraida Sánchez Oliva and Blanca Acosta*
Design and Illustration: *Julio A. Mompeller*

INSTITUTO CUBANO DEL LIBRO
Editorial JOSÉ MARTÍ
Publicaciones en Lenguas Extranjeras
Apartado 4208, La Habana, Cuba

ISBN: 959-09-0050-X
Depósito Legal: M-39986-1995
Imprime: S.S.A.G., S.L.
MADRID (España)

TABLE OF CONTENTS

PROLOGUE

Cuban music, in all of its many forms, has been the subject of an increasing number of studies over the past few years. Several books have been published; tracing the development of composers and performers; compiling periods and genres; not to mention the historical and analytical works, or the reference books. However, much remains to be researched to fully document the wide and rich development of our music over the centuries. Hence the significance of this book by journalist Olga Fernández. The title, Strings and Hide, reflects the special cultural blend that makes Cuban music unique.

Strings and Hide treats a broad range of topics, making it a valuable compendium of names, dances, genres, instruments. It brings to life such trovadores as Chicho Ibáñez, Juan el Pandero (The Tambourine), Angel Almenares, Sindo Garay, Manuel Corona, Blanquita Becerra, Cucho el Pollero (The Chicken Man), Teresita Fernández, Pablo Milanés, and Ñico Saquito; the immortal Matamoros Trio, the legendary Septeto Nacional; outstanding trumpet players such as Félix Chapottín; the first songs and dances of the island; the criolla guitar, the trova of Virgilio, a classic sonero; Miguelito Cuní; folk dancer Nieves Fresneda; and master guitarist Leo Brouwer. Also featured are the Eastern organ, the Cuban rumba, the changüí, the danzón, the sucu-sucu, the sung décima, the tumba francesa, the tonadas trinitarias, *the* batá *drums, the National Folklore Group, Epiphany, Afro-Cuban Festival, and carnival. Unfolding before us is the fusion of Spanish and African cultures, with a dose of French-Afro-Haitian contributions, all taking shape in a new form of artistic expression enriched by contemporaneous contributions.*

African and Hispanic elements, along with traces of native Indian influence early on, had merged into the island's distinctive music by the 19th century. But it is in the 20th that this music really took hold, with a dazzling array of new genres and performance styles.

Olga Fernández methodically researched this rich musical heritage, which has taken on increasing importance with the years. Her book is a valuable contribution to knowledge about the music which has played such a significant role in the Caribbean, Latin America, North America, and in fact the world.

Fernández, as journalist-turned-musicologist, gives us a series of straightforward pieces illuminating numerous topics and individuals. The eye-witness narratives of such a broad range of our islands's musical personalities provide a valuable foundation for new research and approaches to the life and work of these jongleurs and trovadores. *Her journalistic style in no way detracts from the poetic halo that has always surrounded these admirable creators.*

Today popular music is on the rise all over the world. In America, Africa and Europe (and parts of Asia such as Japan) the radio waves, television screens, concert halls and theaters are filled with a wide range of new music. Musical trends such as pop, rock, and other similar rhythms of all kind are sharing the stage with Caribbean beats, often from Cuba. The best representatives of the salsa *movement, mixing different tropical sounds, are heard around the world. Thanks to Cuban and Caribbean musicians, our nations have taken their place on the international artistic scene. There's no doubt that the demand for our music is growing. And so is the need for information about our musicians.*

The roots, growth and current developments of these cultural expressions are of interest to more and more people. But the available literature is inadequate. Hence the value and importance of books such as this.

In no way should this work by Olga Fernández be considered a musicology treatise, history, or composite picture of Cuba's music and musical composers. Her intentions were to bring together chronicles and interviews about our music, accompanied by narrative to make the whole coherent. This was done with an eye to the immediate and longer-term needs such information could be expected to meet. The result is a unique combination of historical data and personal sketches of our native musicians.

HELIO OROVIO[1]

[1]Musicologist and critic, author of the *Diccionario de la música cubana* (Cuban Music Dictionary), Havana, Editorial Letras Cubanas, 1981. "—Ed."

INTRODUCTION

This collection of articles aims to trace the flow of Cuban music from its twin sources: the Spanish and the African.

The pieces span a broad range; from the words of *sonero* Chicho Ibáñez, over a hundred years old, to descriptions of dances as old as the *tumba francesa*, the *contradanza*, the *danzón*, and the *changüí* guantanamero, origin of the *son*[1]; from the story of the adventure-filled life of the first Santiago *trovador* and of Ñico Saquito, father of the *guaracha*, to the exciting description of the songs and dances of Cuba's oldest *comparsa*, descended from a *Carabalí cabildo* and of the traditional drum of the island's Black slaves.

Taken together, a survey of the folk music of the Antilles and the Caribbean, rested in Cuba for centuries, and nurtured from one generation to the next.

Also included in this volume are articles on the founder of the *criolla* song, such as Sindo Garay, Manuel Corona and Miguel Matamoros, as well as the *Nueva Trova* Movement, born from the Revolution and which, without forgetting its roots, created new styles and melodies consistent with the changing times.

---

[1]Italics are used when referring to the Cuban rhythm. "—Ed."

Some of these works have not been published before. Others originally appeared in the magazine *CUBA Internacional*, but they all speak of the common features of our folklore which help to shape the music that has made extraordinary contributions to the universal culture, that had and has, jointly with the great changes occurred in the Cuban nation, a historic base in the people's conscience.

OLGA FERNÁNDEZ

A Hundred Years in the Life of a Singer

The rare and complex personality of Chicho Ibáñez brings together ancestral cultural features that range from the plucking characteristic of guitar players of medieval, Renaissance and Baroque Spain, to the particular rhythmic development of those who played the Guinean balaphon and the Bantu kimbila; from the Arab melismata, and the Andalusian street vendor, to the guaguancó chorus; from the fluourishing Cabezón's variations, to the Passacaglias of a bolero singer like Sindo Garay or a bolero-son singer like Miguel Matamoros; from the special elements of the lyricism of a Guarionex Garay and a Benny Moré, to the unmistakeable tonality of an enkanikó abakuá.

Odilio Urfé

ALLOW me to introduce Chicho Ibáñez, the oldest *trovador* in Cuba and perhaps in the world, the solo singer for whom a *tres* is all that's needed to produce the most extraordinary Cuban *son*.

Allow me to show you a stubbornly happy man who lives as though he were never going to die. Because not everyone lives to be a hundred, as José Ibáñez did, with his vital energies intact, without showing the ravages of time.

Enduring creator of the song with the catchy chorus, Chicho Ibáñez, even after a century, keeps his listeners on the edge of their seats, as he strikes his tres and lets loose with that ancient voice, so loud and strong it makes many think there's a microphone hidden somewhere.

Chicho Ibáñez is always ready to improvise a *son*, and when it comes to attending a recital, honoring his century-long career as a sonero or granting an interview, true to *trovador* form, he laces his replies with songs.

So that, at noon on this day early in the year, after the photo sessions, Chicho in the distance from a narrow street in Old Havana heading toward the Cathedral, where I wait; Chicho, stopped by passers-by, his impecable brown suit with the shiny medals, Chicho, finally seated in front of me, begins to recite his most famous *sones* to illustrate the story.

WHO SAYS THE *SON* IS OLD?

"Whoever told you that the *son* is old told you wrong. What's old is the changüí, which I played with picks, because the thumb-nail technique of playing the tres wasn't known yet."

Chicho says he acquired his taste for the *son* in Manzanillo, Oriente province, and it stayed with him when he came to Havana in the twenties. At that time, the Habanero Sextet—to which he sold many of his compositions for a peso—made his first recordings popular. According to those who knew them at that time (there are very few still living) his *sones* were the rage of Havana. He bears this out saying he came into the world with this music, and like the music he came to stay in Cuba, he's not leaving either.

"In 1906 I wrote *Pobre Evaristo*, my first *montuno*: a *tonada* or tune of three or four words and a repeated phrase I stuck on as a chorus. At that time I worked at whatever turned up: foreman, mechanic, driver, electrician and bricklayer, although my real profession was sonero at parties and serenades. My whole life was a coming and going from one province to another, arriving and leaving at the end of the month, when everyone liked my work; the way time passes, I knew I had to live in a hurry, without sinking roots anywhere, always with my tres over my shoulder, as though it were a tent."

It's as though Chicho were ageless. We always hear it said that when you're old and must die, many things bear down on you: a great anguish or melancholy. In Chicho, it's a vibrant hope, marvelous emotion, perhaps because the best that he's said, he's said with songs.

LIFE IS PHENOMENAL!

"Because life is many things: work, luck, friendship, health, love problems, struggle. But no one can deny that if I put this to music, it's easier to take, and what's more, I know that many say I was unhappy in love, perhaps because of some of my compositions or because I'm so ugly but now you see, I have ten children, one hundred seven grandchildren, twelve great-grandchildren, and five great-great grandchildren. and although it's true I was happy, I was also unlucky. Here, listen to this son:

> Yo era dichoso, sufrir yo no sabía,
> todo era dicha en el mundo para mí.
> Todo era dicha, placer, alegría,
> hasta que te conocí.
> (I was happy, I didn't know what suffering meant. / Everything was good luck for me, / everything was happiness, pleasure, joy / until I met you...)

"And that's where the verse breaks off."

"Now do you believe that life is phenomenal?"

BECAUSE I WAS REALLY GOOD

Chicho Ibáñez has the honor of being, after the late Sindo Garay and Emiliano Blez, the dean of the traditional trova, and even more so of the son. But he's also Cuba's oldest militia-man and the oldest Playa

Girón[1] fighter. And when he's asked how it's possible that he would go out to fight at his age, he responds with the most loving of his smiles: "because I was really good and they had to take me," and he shows his honor diploma attesting to his participation as a member of Bon 14 (Battalion 14).

"Girón was the biggest thing that could happen to me to complete my life. I remember, since my memory is very precise, that they began to drop rockets on the beachhead which we attacked, and I was going forward and going forward, without giving in to the cowardice that always tries to mess with you. A little later, when we cleaned up all that mercenary stuff, Fidel[2] congratulated us without knowing that in the ranks of the battalion there was a stubborn old man, 86, whom they couldn't convince to stay home."

IT COULD HAVE SOMETHING TO DO WITH WOMEN

Once a trovador friend said to me: "We sing in sad moments, when we feel wounded by a woman, or when we're happy. We also sing to Cuba, to her flag, to the palm tree, to the invasion of Maceo and the victory of Girón."

Now Chicho tells me: "I have sung to all the heroes of my country, just think, in all the different periods; to love for Cuba and for a woman... I know José Martí said:

> *¿De mujer?*
> *Pues puede ser*
> *que mueras de su mordida;*
> *pero no empañes tu vida*
> *diciendo mal de mujer."[3]*

[1]Bay of Pigs, scene of the first defeat of imperialism in Latin America. "—Ed."

[2]Fidel Castro, President of the Council of State and of the Council of Ministers.

[3]José Martí, *Versos Sencillos* (Short Poems), Havana, Ediciones La Tertulia, 1961, p. 49.

17

(Woman / you may die of her bite / but don't mar your life / speaking ill of her.)

"All that is true, but sometimes there's no alternative."

THE MOST SUBLIME

To make his poetry sing in an authentically Cuban voice, Nicolás Guillén chose the *son* form. To relate "the most sublime to exhilarate the soul," Abelardo Barroso, unforgettable sonero, perpetuated it in *Suavecito* (Easy). To improve it in a unique way Chicho Ibáñez needs three pairs of high-pitched cords, skillful hands, and the outsize voice that plays with the chorus in its own special way.

"Let me tell you, this *son* business was like a sickness here in Havana when it caught on. It is said that the first sextet was that of the Standing Army in the time of the *Tiburón* (Shark)[4]. What's true is that the groups had Havana in their back pockets, and from then on tres sextets were formed.

"Though I belonged to some groups in Santiago de Cuba and to the Estudiantina de Gabino, in Guantánamo, most of the time I sang alone, because I'm a guy on the move and I can't feel tied down to a group. My *son* entitled *Luis Toledano* dates from that time in Guantánamo. It turns out that a fearsome man lived there who threw himself into the Guaso river with a bicycle with a propeller and even a little boat on the wheels. What happened is that when there was little wind that bicycle was a sled, but when the river rose, Toledano ended up on the bank with two or three ribs broken. Now you tell me if that man didn't deserve a *son* like this:

> *Luis Toledano se cree que el agua es tierra,*
> *le voy a formar la guerra para que no patine más...*
>
> (Luis Toledano thinks water is land / I'm going after him so that he doesn't skate any more...)

[4]José Miguel Gómez, president in the pseudo republic. His term covered from 1909 to 1912.

Chicho Ibáñez, the oldest Cuban trovador

And then he belts out the verse that made Luis more famous than his ingenious bicycle.

Chicho is right when he says that he needs more than one day to talk about his life. Because this composer of more than 300 *sones*, who went through a militia school in 1960, who was awarded the Raúl Gómez García Order for his more than thirty years dedicated to art, who today carries with him a trophy attesting to his one hundred years, who still brings art to the most remote corners of Cuba, cannot possibly be summed up in a few pages.

And because, in addition, Chicho Ibáñez has the rare virtue, shared by children and poets, of talking about the future as something that can be known.

CUBA Internacional. February 1976

JUAN EL PANDERO

THEY say the first trovador of Santiago de Cuba was a mulatto named Juan, who played the tambourine in the Colored militia Band created at the beginning of the 19th century by a Frenchman named Dubois. He had an attractive voice, which he accompanied with his guitar in *tonadillas*, those short musical pieces that made him popular at parties and serenades.

It's also believed that Juan *el Pandero*'s repertoire included some compositions of Esteban Salas (1725-1803), first great master of Cuban music, and that he also sang *boleros* in the Spanish style so representative of that period. He'd seize any opportunity to go to the French theater on Santo Tomás Street, to enjoy the tonadillas of Madame Belot or La Clarais, which would have an important influence on his style.

At first Juan's popularity was due to his way of playing the tambourine—now with the palm of his hand, then short blows with the fingertips, or slow friction, then quick strokes. But he was soon noted for his fine manners, and his exquisite way of treating ladies. His silky trovador voice did the rest. With this combination it was to be expected that his love adventures would end tragically.

One evening he was challenged to a duel by José Utrera, the band's clarinet black player. The facts point to a woman in the middle. Juan's dagger won out. He was charged with murder, and the spot where Utrera fell was called from then on Clarín Street. The efforts of the most influential friends of the colonial government got nowhere: Juan was condemned to the gallows and executed on August 13, 1814, at the same hour that Utrera had died.

Several months later, some highly respected Santiagueros who had been periodically travelling abroad agreed that they had seen *El Pandero* in Jamaica, and that he had confessed that the execution has been a hoax. By then, street improvisation had produced this ditty:

> *Ya murió el Pandero,*
> *déjalo morir,*
> *que del Paraíso,*
> *volverá a salir.*

> (Now El Pandero has died, / let him die, / from Paradise itself, / he will leave again.)

CUBA Internacional. March 1976

THE TIVOLÍ SPELL

T HE *pasapié* and the contradanza were played for the first time at the Tivolí, a thatch and limestone theater built at the end of the 18th century in Santiago de Cuba by the French seeking refuge during the Haitian Revolution.

The new arrivals chose the steep Loma del Intendente hill for their cabaret with its royal palm dressing rooms, a real novelty for the Santiago residents.

Every night, the orchestra directed by Monsieur Dubois played light music to accompany the beautiful soprano Madame Clarais. The style was even lighter when Madame Pufort come on stage. She used the artifices of dance to reveal something more than an ankle to her all-male audience.

As time passed, that part of the city came to be called the Tivolí district. Fire or an earthquake destroyed the French theater. All that remained of its old splendor was the name.

The Tivolí district was the birthplace of the cabildo of the Carabalí Olugo, a fraternal institution of the black slaves, developing out of the carnival tradition.

The spell cast by that theater kept many trovadores and poets born in its surroundings faithful to its tradition. The district was home to many of the most famous members of the *trova mayor* and the most charming serenades made their debuts in its streets.

CUBA Internacional. March 1980

DANCING, *CRIOLLO*-STYLE[1]

T HE first dance craze in Cuba was the contradanza. Introduced by the French settlers from Haiti at the end of the 18th century, it took hold as the great novelty in the grand salons and the little
schools or academies of dance where those of few resources, "young
men and ladies with few responsabilities, go together to pass away
the evening."

There is a description of the customs of Villa de San Cristóbal in
Havana, pre-dating the introduction of the contradanza by two centuries. It says that the dances and entertainments of Havana are gra-
cious and extravagant; the former still show the crudeness and low
level of culture of the natives, while the latter reveals the scarcity and
lack of resources of a population just beginning to advance.

At that time, there were only four musicians at the village; given the
extraordinary enthusiasm for dancing, they could not meet the demand, even though their fees were stiff. There was a violinist from
Malaga, a clarinet player from Lisbon, a violoncellist from Seville and
vihuela player Micaela Gómez, a free black from Santo Domingo.

Besides providing their transportation and giving them a share of the
wine at the party, the musicians also expected a tip in the form of a
full plate of everything put on the table.

[1]If publication is not indicated, the text is unpublished. "—Ed."

Olga Fernández

A report published in *El Aviso* in December 1805, describes a dance
hall with rows of *taburetes* for the ladies and gentlemen, although the
gentlemen usually remained standing as they waited for the master of
ceremonies—solemnly aware of the importance of his office—to give
the signal. Then they could contend for the ladies' favor, a minuet or
a contradanza. The reporter notes that by the third contradanza, the
dancers were already moving restlessly through the hall, the jugs of
sangría, *zambumbia* and *agualoja* refreshments of that time were
being downed, as dancers fortified themselves to keep going. During
intermission, there were *zapateos*, *boleros* and guarachas, and, if
the gathering were not a particularly distinguished one, there would
be loud songs and libertine couplets.

La guabina, a very popular Cuban guaracha, was always featured in
the repertoire of the mulatto girls, whose beauty reigned over those
dances, and whose elegance competed with the impeccable linen
waistcoats of the men, who, though sweating in the heat, did not
dare take off their cloth hats.

Also frequenting the dance halls were the young *criollos* of noble
descent who, bored with balls and evening get-togethers, sought out
the excitement and driving rythms of the blacks'orchestras. Some
contradanzas tended to be catchier when a black band played them,
because they—unlike the white musicians—did not just follow the
score, but added their own special twists and flavor.

San Pascual Bailón, which dates from 1803, is the first contradanza
criolla, the forerunner of the dance developed by Manuel Saumell and
Ignacio Cervantes, along danzón lines. The dance lasted about an
hour, some up to three; they could even go on all night, with the
musicians working in shifts. But not the dancers—they kept going
until they heard the cannon announce daybreak, the time parties had
to end.

Antonio de las Barras y Prado, writing in *La Habana a mediados del
siglo XIX* (Havana in the middle of the 19th century), says that every
Sunday of the years dances were held in the halls of the Escauriza
Café, located across from the Tacón Theater, and on the Alameda de
Isabel II, today the Paseo de José Martí.

"But these dances," he notes, "which when I arrived on the Island[2]
(1852) were attended by women obviously under the firm control of

[2]It refers to Cuba. "—Ed."

24

their parents and family friends, today are visited by brash and bold women who have ruined all the charm of their mysteries."[3]

Many contradanzas were written to be played and heard in concerts. In the fifty-plus most outstanding compositions of Saumell, father of Cuba's distinctive musical identity, there are no two pages alike. The rythmic and melodic creativity of his contradanzas and *danzas criollas* are astonishing. They gave rise to the *habanera*, the danzón, the *guajira* and the *clave* together shaping the most enduring elements of Cuban music.

[3]Antonio de las Barras. *La Habana a mediados del siglo XIX*, Madrid, Imprenta de la Ciudad Lineal, 1925, p. 89-90.

THE GUITAR

A trovador was once asked what the guitar meant to him. He answered, "that although it was as capricious as a woman, he couldn't get by without her." A talented woman composer who was at his side could not just let that go by and said, "for me, the guitar is the most intimate when I compose; it fits itself to the words like a river to the riverbed. It's a confident instrument, with sonorities that cannot be repeated. A miniature orchestra."

Capricious or faithful, the guitar, natural instrument of the *trova*, second voice of the trovador at parties and serenades, turns out to be the most effective ingredient in this infallible recipe: to make a good trova you have to put in some voice, guitar, and a lot of feeling.

In the 18th century there were small guitar and mandolin groups in Santiago de Cuba. Often, a hollow pumpkin with many cracks in it was the other instrument they used, to liven up a party. Unlike the piano, the guitar did not know the ostentation of the great salons, the exquisite orchestral sonorities, nor the opera. It was the instrument acompanying popular dances and evening gatherings, and since its birth in Spain, it has belonged to the masses. But the vihuela and guitar sailed with the *conquistadores* to the New World, and they accomodated themselves to the criollos, who needed to express their feelings of nationality through *décimas* and songs. And the guitar and tres travelled the countryside and the cities, along with the tres, the bandore and the lute, identifying with the peasants.

The guitar, the trova instrument

This string instrument, with the most complete harmonic possibilities, with full sonority when it's made with the artesan's love and mastery, was known in Cuba from the time of the Spanish conquest. But the criolla guitar was not made here until the beginning of the 19th century. First, the wave of French immigrants who fled the slave rebellion led by Toussaint L'Ouverture in nearby Haiti had to arrive on Cuba's eastern shores, bringing with them coffee cultivation, the minuet and the rigadoon. They also brought Monsieur Alexis, a taciturn and gloomy little man, cellist for the comic opera company, and knowledgeable in the art of making string instruments.

One fine day Monsieur Alexis, timid by habit and solitary by avocation, in one of his frequent strolls along the steep streets of Santiago de Cuba, struck up a friendship with a black cabinetmaker, a fan of the French comedy who had his shop a few blocks from the theater. Perhaps out of admiration for Juan José Rebollar's excellent work with all kinds of precious woods, the Frenchman decided to teach him his skills in building top quality instruments.

With time, the instruments made in Rebollar's shop—true works of art which were bought only by criollos and wealthy Spaniards, given their high prices, were in great demand that went beyond the eastern region to finally spread across the entire island.

Since these first criollo guitars were exclusively owned by a social sector cut off from the true trova, which had already been born with the patriotic songs of natural composers, some of the workers and most able apprentices of Rebollar's shop began to make them secretly. With replicas of the models used by the cabinetmaker, tens of criollo guitars were made and sold at low prices to the trovadores of the Tivolí, Los Hoyos and other Santiago districts. Years later, they were the scene of the many *peñas*[1] where trovadores sang the genuine Cuban bolero with a passion that extends to our own time.

CUBA Internacional. June 1974

---

[1] Gathering place for informal performances. "—T."

WHERE THE AUTHENTIC BOLERO IS SUNG

"SILENCE in honor of the trova, silence please," asks the presiding host, and the audience—regulars, passers-by—settle into their seats: "the trova is going to begin."

In this colonial house with brass-studded doors and lanterns, located in the center of Santiago de Cuba, on the same street where José María Heredia, the first great national poet was born, the festivities quiet down as the trovadores go up to the platform and take their taburetes.

A guitarist with an impassive face begins to pick the chords with unusual force, searching for new arpeggios in the indtroduction to the bolero and, at just the right moment, the *voz prima* ("first" voice) of Jústiz and the *segundo grave* (low "second" voice) of Castillo intone the melody.

They sing only three numbers. Then comes a quartet, and then a trio. Bello Día, a little old man with a pointed beard, gratifies a lady with *La guinda* (The Cherry) by Eusebio Delfín. The *Casa* is filling up and the audience demands more: *Sublime obsesión* (Sublime obsession) by Adams, *El peregrino* (The Pilgrim) by Portela. The claves are struck more and more in this bolero which has something of the *son* in the chorus.

In the rear, the small curtain and the sign saying "the trova without a drink gets stuck"—which many trovadores deny. On the walls, two greats of the genre: Sindo Garay and Manuel Corona, in green, yellow, and cinnamon. In a corner, Almenares and his guitar, and Márquez, with a conspiratorial gesture, inviting the more fortunate visitor: "Come and listen to this song." Then a duet lets out with unanimous feeling:

> *Quiero morder tus labios difamantes*
> *y castigar así lo que han hablado.*
>
> (I want to bite your lying lips / and so punish that which they have said.)

Almenares, who today is partying for no particular reason, pulls off the most unexpected notes, while Márquez confesses: "I am singing without wanting to, but this is my fate. Inspiration comes when I least expect it, and if I stop singing I will die." And when someone asks, "What do you feel when the trova performs one of its songs," it is Dr. Fonseca, physician and composer, who responds: "So many things are felt... your pressure goes up, drops, and for me, who has never had a voice for singing, it is like an intimate homage, something that can be said with just these words: I feel like a human being."

HERE'S VIRGILIO

They say that when Virgilio Palais set up his little shop "Aquí está Virgilio" (Here's Virgilio) on Heredia Street, in the fifties, the trova was singing without guitars to a limited public: the drivers from the Céspedes Park taxi stand.

Mariano Carbonell *(Perete)*, president of the Casa de la *Trova*, tells part of the story: "Virgilio was a cigar maker, one of the best, and also a trovador from the Tivolí neighborhood. He had an excellent, strong voice, really resonant; you have to hear it.

"In those years, Ramón Márquez and I, already retired, used to stop by his store and, just while passing through, sing, very softly, a couple of old songs. One time, a driver wanted to celebrate his birthday. He brought along a bottle of rum and the music took off. Almenares showed up with his guitar, we started singing loud, Heredia Street was filled with people, and they applauded. From that day on there was a large audience, since word spread that at Virgilio's they were singing trova. Cucho *el Pollero*, Miguel Angel Jústiz, Augusto and Manolo Castillo, and for the first time and thanks to Virgilio, the Santiago trovadores got together in one place."

Manolo Castillo, member of the Casa board of directors, tells Perete:

"Virgilio's store was just off to the side of this Casa. Painted on the wall are the stave of *La lira rota* (The Broken Lyre), his favorite song.

"Some years after the triumph of the Revolution, the Council of Culture of this province gave us the key to the place and, on July 28, 1968, we opened the Casa de la Trova. It's open every day, morning, noon and night. Perete, Márquez, Cucho, Jústiz and I make up the management and you better believe we work hard because we also have a radio spot, television programs and tours around the province that include performances out in the sugar fields. Although we're retired from other jobs, there's no one who can make us leave this one: the trovador who stops singing grows sad and soon dies."

THE TIMES OF THE GREAT *TROVA*

When the typically Cuban element began to make itself felt in criollo music, that music was still heavily influenced by several European styles such as the stage tune, the Spanish bolero and the Italian lyric. The songs were practically light opera and every trovador felt like an opera tenor.

At the end of the 19th century, the bolero's form, melody and style became more clearly defined through the patriotic songs of such spontaneous composers as Simón Nápoles *(Baracoa)*, who was a major in the Liberation Army, as well as interpretations of the *bolero* by the first Santiago trovadores: José Sánchez *(Pepe)*, Eulalio Limonta, Sindo Garay, Emiliano Blez. But of them all, it was Pepe Sánchez, a tailor from the Los Hoyos neighborhood who, in 1885, composed the first bolero with two stanzas and thirty-two beats, the authentic Cuban bolero that set the standard for those who followed him.

"When I was still in short pants, Pepe Sánchez was already famous as a trovador, guitarist and teacher. He was the precursor, the one who taught Sindo Garay, Villalón, Rosendo Ruiz, Cortina, and other greats of our trova. With Sindo, Cuban *son* came of age," says Márquez.

IT WOULD BE EASIER TO LEARN A WALTZ

Before, during the pseudorepublic, it was not possible to bring the Santiago trovadores together in a set place. Each group had its neighborhood: the Tivolí, Los Hoyos, Marte Square. Ar serenade time and during carnival, the trova went all over the city.

The starting point for the serenades could be the cafés Baltabarín or El Lirio Blanco. The best ones happened on the eve of a birthday, to greet the dawn in the home of the person being honored and join the party, where there was always *ciruelón*, goat and *congrí* or yam with boiled codfish.

Eugenio Portuondo remembers:

"At the serenades we sang boleros, habaneras and criollas, depending on the occasion. If the idea was to win over a lady, we had to include the most deeply felt song, often our own composition; and, if it was the birthday of a trovador or his lady, we gave the bolero more of a beat. In those years the *trova*'s song was practically a capriccio and few could do it. It was easier to learn a waltz."

LISTEN TO THIS BOLERO

It could be one by Pepe Sánchez, Friol, Figarola or Banderas or maybe Sindo. Those who inhabit this casa have their own and of course, it's good. And although nearly a century may go by between one bolero and another, the inspiring subjects are always the same: love, women, country, that is, everything that's marked men's lives for good or evil.

Angel Almenares, guitarist and composer, with an excellent voice, comes up with this explanation of the events that give rise to the bolero:

Aquí está Virgilio shop, located on Heredia Street

"We trovadores sing at sad times, when we feel hurt by a woman, or when we're happy. We also sing to Cuba, to Oriente and believe it or not, when we sing the favorite composition of one of our dead comrades we feel the place fill up with his presence: because they all have something of us. And though it seems strange, so long as there's life we'll sing to it and, when death comes, we sing to that too. We have a mutual agreement inherited from tradition: we sing the favorite song of the dead trovador in his honor guard and when his body is lowered into the grave."

LIFE IN MEMORIES

It's eleven o'clock at night, and the host announces that it's quitting time; the audience leaves the Casa; some go down Heredia Street and others head for Céspedes Park. The trovadores put out the lamps, close the big doors and leave to get their rest.

Tomorrow they'll come back to this house again, which makes them re-live something of their lives through memories. When they learned their guitar chords from the masters and practiced secretly to go out serenading, or when they had to hide their instruments where they worked as apprentices, to go out carousing later behind the old folks' backs, who did not want them to be artists. Not everyone had the luck to work in a barbershop or as a tailor or cigar maker; in those jobs they could sing all the time.

Because, despite the years, they are still motivated to keep singing, their music is a spontaneous testament to this secular fraternity called trova which, in Oriente, is now practically immortal.

CUBA Internacional. September 1973

INVIOLABLE PACT

IF you ask an old trova composer or singer what his favorite subjects are, he's sure to say women, love, homeland and death. Angel Almenares, nearly eighty years old, guitarist and composer of the Santiago de Cuba trova, prefers the subject of death.

"Singing to those who die fulfills a long-standing pact. Each one of us has a favorite composition, and that's the one sung to the person who dies in his honor guard and when he's lowered into the grave. Ramón Márquez and I are the duet who commit ourselves most to this sad task; it's hard and very sad to sing for the last time to the comrades who have shared our lives for so many years. But this final respect must be paid, though we may be crying inside. We sang *La bayamesa* (Woman from Bayamo) to Sindo, *La lira rota* to Virgilio Palais, and *Olvido,* the song that made him famous, his favorite, to Miguel Matamoros.

"Sometimes there are inviolable pacts between two trovadores calling for one of them, the one who survives the other, to sing at the latter's funeral. That's what happened when Toronto died, a phenomenal guitarist with a voice that could be heard blocks away. That day Ñico Escudero, who was supposed to sing to him, was out of Santiago, and he had to return quickly to keep his promise, even though he could not finish the song: his voice broke with emotion."

About Angel Almenares, they say that when he felt he was dying, he asked for pencil and paper, and right there wrote *Cajón de muerto* (Coffin).

Angel Almenares, guitarist and composer of the Santiago de Cuba trova

Ya no me importa mi dolor presente,
Ya no me importa mi dolor pasado

(Now this moment's pain doesn't matter, / now the pain of my past doesn't matter.)

It turns out that that afternoon Almenares had sung at a party and, when they paid him, he went to the market and ate a plate of cold liver, Italian-style. No one knows if he did it on a whim or because he was really hungry; what is certain is that afterwards he felt so bad that he took to his bed and a few hours later his friends held that Almenares would die.

El porvenir lo espero indiferente,
lo mismo es ser feliz que desgraciado.

(I await the future indifferently, / Happy or sad, it's all the same.)

At first, Almenares the guitarist could not do the music and just wrote the lyrics. According to him, he felt like a fugitive from life and was even ready to give it up.

Sólo ambiciono de fastidio yerto,
cansado ya de perdurable guerra,
acostarme ya en mi cajón de muerto,
dormir en paz debajo de la tierra.

(Longing now only for dull rigidity, / tired now of everlasting war, / to lie down in my coffin, / to sleep in peace below the earth.)

But Almenares did not die, and his driving energy is something that must be seen: this fragile old man who, guitar in hand, breaks into the introduction of a bolero or criolla. Because Almenares has his own style of accompaniment; he just needs the pitch and he adds the shadings the song needs "to make it sparkle."

Now, here's Almenares' conclusion about himself:

"One time Gelabert, a Spanish guitarist, heard me play in the town of Cueto, and since I play my own capriccios that are like classic ones, he was surprised. I haven't been carrying this guitar around for fifty-four years for nothing and, though I know something about theory, I'm not like anybody, since it's my own feelings that tell me how to feel the chords, how I should tell a song."

CUBA, Internacional. August 1975

Sindo Garay, Trovador Mayor

T HE truth is that that night back in 1890, the German musicologist Hermann Mikelson felt more curiosity than sympathy towards the boy accompanying Pepe Sánchez. He admired the elegant Santiago tailor for his gifts as a guitarist and composer. For that reason he paid attention when Pepe introduced his disciples to him with these words: "Here I bring you a musical genious."

Despite the merciless heat, the evening gathering was pleasant. Mikelson, accredited in Cuba as his country's consul and a resident of Santiago de Cuba, played a prominent public role and was highly respected by the trovadores and poets who visited his home.

At midnight, Pepe Sánchez interrupted the program to sing, with great skill, one of his own *boleros*, which years later would revolutionize Cuban music. Then, the host wound up the evening by playing some selections from Wagner's Tannhäuser on the piano.

No one then noticed the boy, nearly hidden in a corner of the room, who watched, astonished, as Mikelson's fingers flew over the keyboard.

Used to simple chords and modulations of the songs of the period, he could not take in such brilliant harmony.

Moved to tears, and with the tremendous impact the music made on him reflected on his face, the boy left the room without saying good night to anyone, with the notes of Wagner's *Vivace* threatening to keep him up all night.

A few days later, Mikelson was to see that the words of the master Pepe Sánchez were prophetic. The boy knocked at his door and, with a timid gesture, handed him his song *Germania,* while whispering that he'd composed it in honor of that "guarner" who "doesn't keep still harmonically."

For Mikelson, it was overwhelming to be given this sudden proof that Sindo Garay, the favorite pupil of Pepe Sánchez, really was a musical genius. If he wasn't, what was the explanation for the boy, who did not have the slightest notion of the notes and their arrangement on the musical staff, to have written a song with such a melody and such complicated chromatic language?

THE ACROBAT OF THE GRIÑÁN

In the 1890's, Sindo worked as an acrobat in the Los Caballitos de Griñán Circus. His partner in the act, Emiliano Blez, deceased dean of the traditional trova, sang duets with him at serenades and parties. Once, on tour with the circus, they passed through Puerto Rico, and both visited the Puerto Rican composer Juan Campos. After an enthusiastic greeting and a long talk about the music being played in Cuba then, Campos sang his most famous waltz and then got the Cubans to sing one of Sindo's pieces. For Campos, the second voice and melodic richness of the criolla he heard was delighful. Campos brought out some scored paper to have them write down the music and so preserve it, but, seeing the Cubans break out laughing and return his paper, he asked what was going on. It was Sindo, very embarassed, who explained that they played by ear, and that he'd never written down the music of one of his compositions. Campos' eyes opened wide and he began laughing with them. When they said their good-byes, he pressed their hands affectionately and said: "Boys, never say you don't know music, nobody will believe it."

ONE HUNDRED YEARS IN THE LIFE OF A SINGER

"I was born in Santiago de Cuba on April 12, 1867. *Caray*, how the years have gone by!," said the trovador about to celebrate his hundredth birthday. The fact is that old man in the white *guayabera* and straw hat, standing proud with his cane made of the finest cedar, was part of Cuba itself, as much as the palm tree he praised in one of his criollas.

This man, who had barely learned to read, gave Cuba a whole century of marvelous criollas such as *Guarina* (1912) and *Mujer bayamesa* (1918), the latter better known as *La bayamesa;* and two indisputably lyric poems that are the culmination of his work: *El huracán y la palma* (The Hurricane and the Palm Tree) and *Tardes grises* (Grey Afternoons) (1926).

Among the testimonials about Sindo Garay is that of guitarist Vicente González Rubiera (*Guyún*):

"I knew Sindo when he lived in the La Asunción neighborhood, outside Santiago de Cuba. I remember they told me 'Sindo is building a house in La Asunción, on a little plot of land he bought on the installment plan.' When I got there, no one could tell me where Sindo lived. I called out to him a few times and suddenly I saw him emerge from a patch of weeds shouting, 'Who's looking for Sindo around here?' I didn't see any house, but he took me to a huge wooden box, those used to ship pianolas, and told me to get in. The only thing there was a rocking chair, missing the rocker, and a guitar. I was astonished, and said, 'But Sindo, what are you doing here?' And he answered me in that special way of his, "Here, closer to the music."[11]

In 1896, a year after Cuba's Independence War heated up again, Sindo Garay was getting off the steamship *Avilés* in the port of Havana. It was the first visit to the capital. Ten years later he was back to stay, with an old suitcase and his guitar with German strings. He met Manuel Corona—another great of the trovador's song—in the La Marina Café, near the port.

Years later, Sindo came to prefer the Vista Alegre Café. He greeted the dawn there, singing and drinking a good hit of rum, though he was always sober. Since he was considered the national master of the trova, all of the habitués loved him and shared in his music. "The

[11]Mayra A. Martínez. "Guyún, Trovador Mayor", in *Revolución y Cultura*, (72): August 1978, p.59.

greatest thing I have is being Cuban," he repeated to the point of satiety, and that patriotic feeling spilled over into his songs. Even as a very old man, he kept visiting the downtown Havana Café, singing the second part with his son Guarionex. Those who heard the duet, agreed it was unique in the history of Cuban song. And luckily for Cuba, Sindo lived to be a hundred and two and spent ninety-two of those years composing the best of our music. Starting with *Quiéreme, trigueña* (Love Me, Brunette), the first song he composed at the age of ten.

THE MOST SUNG

La Tarde (The Afternoon), *Perla Marina* (Sea Pearl), *La bayamesa*, *Clave a Maceo* (Clave to Maceo), *El huracán y la palma*, *Tardes grises*, among others, are the favorites of those who sing the traditional songs. But during Sindo's life there were few trovadores who, according to him, performed his numbers well. That, in addition to the fact that a good tenor or baritone voice was required. It was terrible for them to sing before the master. He was that demanding.

Nearly senile, Sindo performed his final serenade. That night he asked those accompanying him to take some photos with him, and then he left for the Plaza de Marte (Marte Square) where the Trova Festival was being held in his honor. He had to be gratified with *El beso adorable* (The Adorable Kiss), a song he never tired of hearing. And after such a warm reception he confessed with an innocent smile: "I don't know, Sindo Garay, old, ugly and squinting, and people always, Sindo here and Sindo there. Sindo's never been more than an old grouch." And these witticisms of his entertained everyone.

SYMBOL OF CUBA

Someone once said that Sindo Garay's *La bayamesa* is our second national anthem. Like *El huracán y la palma*, it glorifies the country's symbols, and *Clave a Maceo* evokes Cuban rebellion.

"All I leave to my country are my songs," he wrote when he felt death near, as his lyric testament.

Cuban musicologist Odilio Urfé says that through his many recordings it could be said that *Tardes grises* is one of the songs where Sindo shows the range of his vocal interpretative art. He states that Sindo constantly surprises with his lyric impressions, loaded with sighing accents, dark and dramatic, but of incalculable beauty and high artistical level. Something similar can be perceived in *El huracán y la palma*, where the lyric-colloquial style (with Guarionex) unleashes onerous tensions of great expressive power. Urfé points out that both were written in the period that reaffirms the national condition of our culture from a militant anti-imperialist position, that is, that of Juan Marinello, enriched with the splendid combination of the *son* and the *danzonización* of the most representative and popular criollas and boleros of our trova repertoire.

Sindo always insisted that "the opera tenor and baritone are the models on which the mode of interpretation for the first and second voices of a trova duet should be based." So many of his creations required close study and a lyrical tessitura.

Because the most surprising thing about this excellent guitarist, who never studied in a school or conservatory, is his natural talent for creating complex songs, complex both in words and melody, such as *La tarde*, which made the master Ernesto Lecuona exclaim that this *bolero* was simply a miracle, a perfect composition, that had no defects, it cannot be surpassed.

When asked about his inspiration, Sindo invariably said: "I sing to love, to women, to the homeland and to death. To everything that inspires me in this beautiful life."

The afternoon in July, 1968 that he died, he was buried in Bayamo. And all the trovadores who went to pay tribute to him sang *La bayamesa*, his favorite song.

To the history of Cuban song, he left his prolific work and a lyric testament carried out in honor of Gumersindo Garay, the greatest trovador.

> Yo le dejo a mi patria, de mi alma el recuerdo,
> porque sé que muy pronto ya me espera el oscuro.

Sindo Garay, Trovador Mayor

Cuando hablen de Cuba en alegres reuniones
y recuerden canciones que los hagan vivir,
que recuerden las mías que sirvieron de guía...

(To my country I leave the memory of my soul, / because I know that very soon the dark awaits me / when they speak of Cuba in joyful reunions / and recall songs that make them live, / let them recall mine that served as a guide...)

Manuel Corona, Author of "Replies"

THE most regular patrons of the La Marina Café, at the corner of Egido and Merced, were trovadores. Behind its broad walnut doors, there was singing at all hours of day and night. It was almost as if time had stopped in the small room with the ostentatious bar and delicate Venetian chairs.

Leaning on a tasteful marble table, a heavy-set mulatto, with Oriental eyes and fine features, strummed the tune of a criolla on his guitar. There were few customers at that time of day, a peaceful time for composing songs.

It was so peaceful that the man, half-asleep, hummed the soaring arpeggios. Just then a small, energetic man came in, practically dragging a large Spanish guitar along with him. They never knew if he came directly from the nearby railway station, or if he was already staying in Havana, though without a permanent address. What's for certain is that he did not know the city. That's how the story is told: that Gumersindo Garay, from Santiago, went straight up to the guitarist's table and suddenly asked him: "Hey, buddy, where can a guy find a good living situation?"

The other man, surprised, raised his head and studied the new-comer. But when he noticed the valuable guitar, he answered, while still running his fingers over his own, "At San Lázaro and Belascoaín, the Vista Alegre Restaurant. You're sure to find what you're looking for there." And with that, he went on with the same task of finding the best melody for his composition.

From that day on, Manuel Corona and Sindo Garay, composers and performers, two of the greats of the Cuban trova, would cultivate a harmless enmity in the music world.

To the masters' duel that waged over thirty years, Cuban music owes a hefty number of compositions, whose high quality has enriched it and made it great.

A WOMAN AND FOUR SONGS

Manuel Corona (Caibarién, Cuba, 1880) was the man who wrote more "replies" than anyone to the other composers of his time. His song *Animada* (Lively) was the reply to *Timidez* (Shy), by Patricio Ballagas; *Gela amada* (Beloved Gela) to *Gela hermosa* (Lovely Gela), by Rosendo Ruiz.

He also applied his talent to the subjects of love, country, and women. *Longina, Mercedes, Santa Cecilia, Aurora, La Alfonsa,* and *La rosa negra* (The Black Rose) are some of the pieces he dedicated to women he had known. And it was a woman, the notable María Teresa Vera, who best interpreted his music. With a song by her teacher Corona, María Teresa made her debut at the age of fifteen. For her, he was "the musical author who best expressed the Cuban soul."

Although she told me that "every time Corona suffered a disappointment, a marvelous inspiration burst forth, to his glory," the truth is that he loved only Mercedes and *Yoya* (Eulogia Real). The other criollas as beautiful as Longina and Alfonsa Rosado, awoke only his deepest admiration.

He met the young Alfonsa Rosado at the home of liberal senator Martín Morúa Delgado. His fleeting relationship with this fascinating woman inspired Corona to write two *boleros: La Alfonsa* and *Las flores del Edén* (Flowers of Eden).

Such is the melodic richness of *La Alfonsa*, written for his "second" voice, that on listening to it, Corona derived another song from it, this one for the "first" voice. These two served as the basis for two more compositions, yielding four songs with different words and melody lines. The four versions of *La Alfonsa* were sung simultaneously, one overlapping the other, by Corona himself, Patricio Ballagas, Rafael Zequeira and María Teresa Vera.

There was never a better quartet, and never was the same woman sung to in four different ways.

Cuban musicologist Ezequiel Rodríguez says that *La Alfonsa* has been Manuel Corona's richest and most developed work, though not his most popular. He thinks that he was thirty or forty years ahead of his time, as regards that song's harmony.

ACCURATE PREDICTION

At the age of eleven, Manuel Corona was a skilled cigar maker, and an excellent guitarist. At that time, the most common jobs for trovadores were cigar maker, tailor and barber. In the La Eminencia cigar factory, an old hand taught Corona to handle a guitar guide practically perfectly. And from La Eminencia, he left every afternoon heading for the most frequented cafés in Old Havana, to earn some money as a trovador.

In 1902, he went to Santiago de Cuba. He was fifteen years old and an excellent "second" voice. In the famous Colón Café in that city, he met Pepe Sánchez, precursor of the trova and creator of the Cuban bolero. The famous guitarist and master set there with Manuelito Delgado and Pepe Banderas, an incomparable trio in eastern Cuba's trova. After listening to some of the compositions of the young man who'd just arrived from Havana, he told him, with prophetic conviction, "You'll be something, Corona." And he was right.

THE SAD FATE OF A *TROVADOR*

Manuel Corona Raimundo wrote songs, *bambucos*, guarachas, claves, habaneras, rumbas and *sones*. At a time when the Cuban song dealt with not only idyllic themes, but also patriotic ones, he wrote *Pobre*

Cuba (Poor Cuba), a virtual denunciation of the corrupt government of Alfredo Zayas, one of those presidents of the pseudorepublic who provoked rebellion and resistence in the people, after their hard-won independence.

The first verse of this song is a good indicator of the marked degree of rebellion arising from the country's frustration, promoted by this composer of songs of independence fighting feeling.

> *¡Pobre Cuba, patriotas cubanos, pobre nación!*
> *Los guerreros que sucumbieron su tiempo perdieron.*
> *De Maceo y Martí de recuerdo queda el nombre,*
> *pues todo lo ha destruido la ambición*
> *de algunos hombres sin compasión.*
> *¡Pobre Cuba, patriotas cubanos, pobre nación!*

(Poor Cuba, Cuban patriots, poor nation! / The fallen warriors were wasting their time. / Of Maceo and Martí, we have their names to remember, / since everything has been destroyed by the ambition / of some merciless men. / Poor Cuba, Cuban patriots, poor nation!)

Manuel Corona, like most of those musical creators, did not put his songs on paper. He shared them with other trovadores, who sometimes made their own contributions to the words or music, in close collaboration, which seemed like nothing so much as a guild.

It often relied on the division of the words, on repetition, stress of an incomplete phrase which was later rounded off by a highly expressive musical phrase. In addition to the four versions of *La Alfonsa*, with *Una mirada* (A Glance), Corona tried two lines of independent songs, with different lyrics for the "first" voice, until the "second" voice went off completely on its own.

Manuel Corona made his songs known at family gatherings and the most frequented cafés in Havana. His guaracha *El servicio obligatorio* (The Draft) won wide acceptance when the draft was imposed in Cuba as a result of the World War II.

With this and other compositions, for which he never received royalties, he fully satisfied the popular conception of the good trovador as a chronicler of his times.

His feverish and impetuous life, the Bohemian society he moved in, left Manuel Corona in the most absolute poverty. This, at a time

Manuel Corona, author of "Replies"

when deep political contradictions were giving rise to intense struggle against the corrupt Republican structure and US interference.

On January 9, 1950, the outstanding musician was found dead in his miserable hut on the Marianao Beach. Behind the dubious El Jaruquito Bar, the musician who had given so much glory to Cuba hid his deep poverty. Poor, forgotten and seriously ill, he died alone, despite the fabulous life's work he had left his country.

A sad death for this trovador whose immense output nourished the root of Cuban musical culture.

CUCHO AND HIS FLYING GUITAR

HOW fantastic that guitar of Cucho *el Pollero*, when he picked it up and slung it over his shoulder, still playing! Then he'd throw it over his head and catch in in mid-air without missing a beat of *Son de la Loma* (They are from the Hill), which he sang like the best of them.

Cucho is a big black guy with the face of a boy. Of a good boy. His voice is slight and gentle, a caressing one. The flying guitar in his hands seems like a jumping small toy.

Since he's a guitarist, Cucho doesn't play bad guitars. And that black guitar with gilded strings must be good; it keeps on flying and still sounds fine.

"I call this guitar my shadow," he says. "I call it that because it follows the song without missing a note."

Before, way before the flying guitar, he was not famous. He did not even have a Casa de la Trova like the one in Heredia Street in Santiago de Cuba, where the bolero, the *son montuno*, and the criolla are sung at all hours.

His real name is Ignacio Bombú. That's what he was called until the day that he did not have a job, not even a guitar to make a living with, and he grabbed some chickens, the best in the coop, and set out to sell them on the streets of Santiago de Cuba.

From that day on he was called Cucho *el Pollero*, and the name stuck.

Ignacio Bambú, Cucho el Pollero

"Then I bought my first guitar," Cucho adds. "I bought it for a few cents. It had a hole in it and a sound like something you'd make on a

51

box codfish is packed in. But old or new, every guitar sounds different. Any carpenter can make a piece of furniture but not a guitar.
Sometimes, it's got a finish like fine furniture, but it's no good. Other
times it's not so pretty, but the trovador falls in love with it, as frivo-
lous as a woman, and he gets the best sound out of it. You've got to
feel a lot of love for a guitar and know it well to get it to sound like it
should.

"Before, the Santiago trova did not have a Casa. We sang all over the
city. That was up to the day we got together at the shop originally
called *Aquí está Virgilio*, on Heredia Street.

"Virgilio was a tall, heavy mulatto who had a lovely tenor voice. He
was from the Tivolí district and I knew him from there. The day a
friend said to me, 'Cucho, come with me to Virgilio's store,' I went
there to greet him. But when I got there I found Perete, Márquez and
Jústiz leaning on the counter, They were singing very softly, and
Virgilio, who was really a nice guy, served a customer, then joined the
group and followed the melody in his 'first' voice.

"Is this a shop or a place for trovadores?" I asked Virgilio. And he,
who was singing *La lira rota*, his favorite song, answered with a
smile, 'I don't know what it is, but I like the singing here.'

"I got into the habit of going to Virgilio's store every day. When I'd
get there, there would already be several trovadores there. One would
bring a new composition, another would ask how this or that passage
was played on the guitar. But we always ended up singing.

"That narrow shop was in a good location. It would fill up with people;
it got so popular that Virgilio sold more merchandise than ever. The
customers came in to hear us sing.

"That's where I began to do the balancing act with my guitar. And
when the Revolution opened the Casa de la Trova, right next to *Aquí
está Virgilio* shop, the whole town knew that on that part of Heredia
Street, singing went on at all hours."

CUBA Internacional. April 1981

THE OLDEST TRIO IN THE WORLD

SIRO and Cueto sang with Miguel Matamoros for the first time on May 8, 1925, Miguel's birthday.

A lot of people got together that night in front of the house of the beloved guitarist, who was celebrating his thirty-first birthday.

Three years later, a certain blond and ruddy figure—that's how he was remembered—attended a performance of the gala at Aguilera Theater in Santiago de Cuba. It was "Mr. Terry," a US impresario combing the island for artists who could help his firm turn a nice profit. Mr. Terry, in the orchestra circle, watched the good trovadores, one after another, impassively. But when Siro, Cueto and Miguel came on, he nearly jumped out of his seat, saying in perfect Spanish to the person next to him: "This trio is wonderful." When the performance ended, the impresario proposed to them that they go to the United States to record with RCA Victor, under the name of the Matamoros Trio.

In July of that same year, the records of the Matamoros Trio reached Cuba, and with them came sudden success, making them the most famous Cuban musical group of the time.

The following year, the Matamoros premiered Miguel's *bolero-son*, *Lágrimas negras* (Black Tears). A new variation of the trova was born: the *son*.

CHARMING POINT

The *son* came to Havana in 1909. It was brought by the trio of Sergio Danger (tres), Emiliano Didull (guitar) and Mariano (*bongo* drums). They were all from Santiago, and members of what was known then as the Standing Army. But the ones who, in the twenties, made this vital root-rhythm of Cuban popular music famous there, were the Habanero Septet.

Twenty years later another trio from Santiago, the Matamoros Trio, would come to the capital, bringing a very curious symbiosis, the bolero. Until then, the Cuban trova followed along the lines of country music or the romantic song. This trio initiated their new aspect by incorporating something livelier in their boleros and montunos.

Musicologist Odilio Urfé has noted that taking the Santiago-inspired *son* as a base, Miguel, Siro and Cueto successfully had cultivated nearly a dozen of the thirteen variants of the Cuban *son* group. It must be added that their repertoire also included habaneras, criollas and generically indentified songs. But, undoubtedly, Urfé added that the eastern-style *son*, with its characteristics (passacaglias that Miguel created with unmatched mastery and Cuban essence) had been the genre that immortalized and popularly identified the Matamoros Trio.

THE MATAMOROS TRIO

Until the moment they got together, Siro, Cueto and Miguel were men who held different jobs, trovadores by avocation. They'd never sung outside their native city.

When they returned in 1928 from the United States, where they had recorded for RCA Victor, they went back to their jobs. Miguel, as a chauffer. A few months went by. One day he was driving his employer's car when they saw a crowd gathered in front of a record store. His employer sent Miguel to buy him the latest hit, and he brought him a record by the Matamoros Trio. After listening to it, the man asked Miguel if anyone in his family was a musician, because the record was of songs by some Matamoros fellows. Later he found out from Miguel himself that the thirty-day leave Miguel had asked for had been to record that record. The next day, the employer gave his driver, Miguel Matamoros, an envelope containing the following note:

"An artist of your extraordinary merit deserves a better fate, and it would not be fair of me to keep you on as my chauffeur."

The letter also included a hundred pesos in cash as a gift. From then on, the Matamoros Trio dedicated themselves completely to making their music known.

Miguel learned to play the tres with the noted musician Augusto Punete Guillot, a mysterious figure who later deserted the Standing Army and died a bandit. Siro preferred the tango, although he knew some of Miguel's songs by heart, and Cueto used to accompany Matamoros on the guitar.

In Los Hoyos and the Tivolí, the trovador neighborhoods, they liked to go out serenading. Often groups left from some café to go around Santiago at midnight.

On one of those endless nights, Miguel was walking through the city with a group of friends. While singing beneath the balcony of a woman, he heard a young girl ask her mother, "Where are the singers from, mama?" And the mother, to get her to go to sleep, said without thinking: "They're from the Loma neighborhood." And that's how the famous *Son de la Loma* was born.

Miguel Matamoros was a true creator of the people. At the age of seven he wrote his first bolero, and at fifteen played the guitar with such skill that he was asked to play at parties and serenades. Everything out of the ordinary, he'd set to music. His compositions grew out of daily happenings. His musical output came to nearly two hundred titles, all unmistakably Cuban. His interpretative style was ahead of his time.

MOURNING FOR A *TROVADOR*

Rafael Cueto maintains, proudly, that the Matamoros Trio was the world's most enduring. They were together for thirty-seven years. "They rehearsed, triumphed and retired together."

Once, when the trio was a septet, one of its members was absent for several days. Curious, Miguel asked what was going on in that musician's life. They told him he'd gotten involved with a woman and was trying to earn extra money on the side. If Matamoros did not raise his pay, he would not return to the group. Matamoros refused ... and from that incident, the guaracha-son *El que siembra su maíz* (He who sows his corn) was born.

El que siembra su maíz was the song that made them really popular. Later would come *Olvido*, *Lágrimas negras*, *Son de la Loma*, *Juramento* (Oath), *Reclamo místico* (Mystic Claim), *Buche y pluma n'má* (A Bluff, That's What You Are), *La mujer de Antonio* (Antonio's Woman) and others. Miguel Matamoros had a large repertoire in addition to other songs such as *La cumbanchera*, by Agustín Lara; *Frutas del Caney* (Caney Fruit) by Félix B. Caignet; *Ausencia* (Absence) by Rodrigo Prats, and others by Benny Moré.

In addition to the Matamoros Trio's frequent trips to Europe, Latin America and the Caribbean, they appeared on television and in films. They made much talk about a film shown in New York, for which they were paid a mere three hundred dollars.

In May, 1969, the Matamoros Trio decided to retire. Siro and Cueto, who lived in Havana, sang again with Miguel only when they visited Santiago de Cuba.

In 1962, Miguel Matamoros wrote his last song. His death, nine years later, occasioned great mourning in Santiago de Cuba. His dearest friends sang the songs of Miguel Matamoros that April afternoon. That's how they complied with the pact of paying respects to dead trovadores with music.

And it was *Olvido*, the song that made him famous, his favorite, that was sung most when Miguel was laid to rest.

FOR MIGUEL

Many times, the Matamoros Trio actually became a septet. Benny Moré sang with them, before becoming the King of Rhythm. Then

The oldest trio in the world

they added other instruments, like Santiago's Chinese cornet, played during the province's carnival season, the horn heard more in Los Hoyos, Miguel Matamoros neighborhood, than any other.

The septet, playing in clubs and roof gardens at several Havana hotels, is remembered as enthusiastically as the Trio. The Trio that never stopped singing as such.

Twenty years after his retirement, Cueto, the only survivor of the Matamoros Trio, still misses those years together. For him, the work of Miguel is so vital that it was not affected by his death. His songs defy time, and they are still sung the same way, losing nothing in originality and freshness. "The most important thing," Cueto said, "is that Miguel is still vital and his compositions are sung in the four corners of the earth. I prefer the way we did them, but taste can't be frozen in a certain period. What's important is that they're sung."

There were few who played the guitar like Miguel Matamoros. Perhaps the one who came closest was Ignacio Bombú, better known as Cucho *el Pollero*, whose life was dedicated to Matamoros' music.

One day they told Miguel there was a trovador in Santiago who imitated his guitar style, and he wanted to meet him.

They came across each other by accident, when the trio was singing in Holguín and Miguel challenged Cucho to show that he was the second Matamoros. After hearing him, he realized that he used the same tones, and his arpeggios were just as convincing as his. And it made him so happy that he hugged Cucho *el Pollero* and told those present that this man was the one who'd gotten closest to his music.

The last time Miguel went out to sing, Cucho accompanied him on the guitar. Miguel was sick then and it was only with great effort that he could stay on his feet.

That night he cried, because he did not have the strength to play his guitar, although, when they went out on the serenade, he did accompany, very softly, one of his most deeply-felt songs.

THE EASTERN ORGAN

PERHAPS the most picturesque spot in Santiago de Cuba is the Taberna de Dolores, where you go to drink beer and dance till you drop to the music of the Eastern Organ.

A door with a raised lintel, walks with splendid murals of the city, a lush colonial patio opening like a fan when it's time to dance, and the organ, that touches everyone present with its inimitable sound of a "transistor radio with bellows." That's the Taberna de Dolores. But the organ is something else again.

Originating in Europe, the organ was most frequently used in the eastern part of Cuba, where it became popular in the 19th century.[1] Polkas and Parisian waltzes were the first rolls of organ music that reached Cuba. Later, the organ's repertoire was expanded to include Cuban musical forms such as the *son*, the guaracha, the bolero, the danzón, the rumba and the cha-cha-chá.

And its pace, relatively slow, nearly liturgical, was livened up with *timbales*, *tumbadora* or *conga* drum, *güiro* or *guayo* and the *cencerro*, all used in the *Golpe de bibijagua* (The Ant's Beat), one of the favorite pieces played by this curious music box.

Two cranks operate the instrument: a small one to manage the tune, and a big one for the bellows. The air goes through the "secret box"

[1]That is why the organ has that name. "—Ed."

that transfers it to the tiny holes punched out on the cardboard (the musical notes), run under a keyboard of sixty-six keys. To operate both cranks, you need more ability than strength, a sense of rhythm, and a lot of endurance.

The music rolls, which last for about a year, are manufactured by two special machines created in Cuba, taking as a guide musical scores for the piano, guitar or saxophone. The number of rolls determines an organ's repertoire, and the number of dancers, how effective its sound is. It has the great advantage of being an orchestra that doesn't need amplifiers, batteries or electricity, just open space and air, lots of air. And the curious virtue of being tuned just before leaving on a truck for the city, or distant places.

IN MANZANILLO THEY DANCE THE SON

The eastern organ is the traditional instrument of this coastal city, gateway to the Sierra Maestra.[2] The exact date the first one arrived in Manzanillo is not known, but the Municipal Archives say that in November 1876 the organ was featured at twenty-two dances in the area. It also appears in official records of the turn of the century, since City Hall clerks were paid out of funds collected at the organ dances.

According to Carlos Borbolla, a composer from Manzanillo, and a member of a family who built these organs, his father began with two, one for his home and another meant to be rented out. Each one cost three hundred pesos, a large sum at the time. Years later, the Borbolla family would make a lot of money with these mechanical devices that played "ground out music", and learned how to mark the musical pieces on rolls.

Carlos himself, author of nearly five hundred piano pieces, also wrote several *organerías*. That's what *sones* for the organ were called. They opened the way for transcribing those curious rolls.

[2]Mountain range located in the eastern part of Cuba. "—T."

The eastern organ

CRANK IT UP AND LET'S DANCE

They say that they were named as soon as they arrived in Cuba, and that they were singled out according to the state of their health and the timber of their sound.

Some travelled better than others, than those that, broken, gather dust in the corner of some house. Those that survive the pounding of impassible roads, rain, and nonstop work, play for nearly half a century. Among them are El Radio (The Radio), weighing in at ten *quintales* (1,250 pounds) with its deep voice, and more than one hundred pieces in a dozen styles in its repertoire. The musicians who handle and travel with El Radio have been with it for more that twenty years, and look after it like a family member.

In addition to El Radio, fussed over by the dancers of Manzanillo, there are others who've enjoyed a productive life and tireless work on the road. After long years they rest in a set place.

There's the one at the Taberna de Dolores, for example, which after a brief pause sounds the gentle notes of a bolero that concludes by turning into a resounding *Son de la Loma*.

"I Refuse to Grow Old"

B LANCA Becerra first danced atop a green baize table at
the age of five, and after that, she became the star of her father's
circus-theater. At nine she crossed the fortified Spanish line from
Júcaro to Morón to take money and medicine to the Cuban independence forces. As a teenager, she performed in Spain in the operetta,
comedy and drama, and at twenty five she began to perform in the
Alhambra, the cathedral of Cuban vaudeville theater. Today, she is
the only Alhambra Theater survivor.[1]

At the age of ninety-five, Blanca Becerra still misses the stage. With
vivacious, laughing eyes, she says she'd give her life to be able to
perform again. And with her still-musical voice, she sings *Po po po*,
the aria of Dolores Santa Cruz, a singular character in *Cecilia Valdés*,
Cuba's best-loved *zarzuela* (operetta).

"Now, I don't want you to get the idea I saw the Morro[2] being built,"
she says with the same Cuban sparkle that made her famous in comedy sketches and monologues. "You might get that idea, if you remember that for 85 years, I worked in the circus, the Spanish zarzuela,
the vernacular comedy, radio, TV, and performed ingénue, comedy
and character roles. The fact of the matter is that when it comes to
the boards, I did it all."

[1]Blanca Becerra died in Havana on October 30, 1985. "—Ed."

[2]Havana's famed 17th century fortress. "—T."

THE HAPPIEST NIGHT

Blanca Becerra's memories are like ants who have lost their way back to the anthill. She knows that she happened to have been born in San Antonio de Vueltas, a small town in central Cuba, right after one of her parents' roving theatrical shows, and that she spent her childhood in wagons riding along poor roads, under circus tents and in slow ferry boats.

She sees herself, tiny and chubby, dancing the danzón and the zapateo on a table "... while Papa collected the Spanish gold coins the audience threw at me." Because she was so busy singing couplets, dancing the waltz on stilts and doing imitations, her parents forgot that she was a little girl who ought to play and go to school: "My parents did all they could to keep me dancing," she says in a tone of living reproach. "They'd buy me dolls only after a good performance. But anyway, the theater I remember with the greatest affection is my father's Estrella Circus-Theater."

The venerable lady with her sweet look and shaky voice, seated in a easy chair in her small, nicely decorated apartment, mixes memories and impossible dreams in her conversation.

On a small table is a round box with a transparent lid that contains her numerous medals. At the center is the Contribution to Cuban Culture award, the one she values most: "Fidel himself pinned it on me. I was so happy that night, really happy. I said over and over that I loved him, and he replied, and I love you, girl. I grabbed his hand very hard."

QUIÉREME MUCHO

In Blanca Becerra's career there is something that is not known to many people, her deep love for composer Gonzalo Roig (see appendix), her husband in the declining years of maturity, and her love for the very popular criolla-bolero Quiéreme mucho (Love me a lot), of which she is co-author with Roig.

"I remember how one day Gonzalo called me to the piano to hum the first part of a song he was composing, and without realizing it, I began to hum a reply to the verse. That was the birth of *Quiéreme mucho*, a song that went round the world....

"I think that for the same reason I love Dolores Santa Cruz, in Roig's zarzuela *Cecilia Valdés*. It's as if he'd written the song for me," she adds with a note of sadness.

"I REFUSE TO GROW OLD"

Clearly, Blanquita (diminutive of Blanca) refuses to be old. She was already over ninety when she left the theater, and now she faces the unusual tranquility of the home.

"My mother predicted I'd live a long life, but I never thought it'd be this long. I refuse to grow old, sometimes I cry because I feel such an urge to dance and sing for my public. But I have to settle for repeating to myself some speeches from plays that I haven't forgotten. I feel less lonely that way."

As she speaks, she handles with consummate flirtatiousness a fan that she used to wield on stage. With her face radiating something invincibly young, she briefly becomes the Blanquita Becerra who was admired by three generations as the top star of the popular Cuban theater.

THE CATHEDRAL OF CUBAN VERNACULAR

The Alhambra Theater, which staged vernacular works for 35 years, housed over 2,000 plays mostly dedicated to political satire. Farces, musical reviews, comedies using stock characters such as the *mulata*, the *negrito* and the *gallego*, respectively, the brown girl, the Black and the Spanish immigrant man, all delighted audiences.

Blanca Becerra, the venerable lady with her sweet look...

After triumphing in Spain as a soprano of a delicate quality of tone, Blanca Becerra arrived at the Alhambra in 1912, and performed there for 23 years.

"The story goes that the Alhambra was for men only, but that's not true at all. The shows we put on there were seen by Havana families and were also staged in short seasons in the Payret and Nacional theaters. I did three shows a day, from Monday through Saturday, and five on Sundays, and the fact is that we never shocked a soul, as some people claim. All we showed were our ankles, much less than what women today display in the street. Really, that was a brilliant period in Cuban theater, because the best actors and directors belonged to the Alhambra."

Blanquita's star roles included *La isla de las cotorras* (Isle of the Parrots), *La casita criolla* (A Little House in the Country) and *Aliados y alemanes* (Allies and Germans), in which she was fired from a cannon into the orchestra. Her talent shone more than once in these works. "It's very important for me that my friends come to see me," she says forcefully, "... that stay for a while. The day I was ninety-five, I felt very flattered, because my last stage companions, the people from the Musical Theater, celebrated with me, and it felt like old times. I sang and danced in the Musical Theater's Alhambra Room, a small replica of the theater in which I spent my career, that is, my life."

CUBA Internacional. September 1982

"I'M THE SONG OF THE CHILDREN"

TERESITA Fernández (Santa Clara, 1930) reaches children with tenderness. A trovador who talks and sings to them about fish and shells, frogs and plants, and who in addition teaches them poetry by Gabriela Mistral and the verses that José Martí dedicated to his little boy, is like a loving teacher who wins children over from her open-air classroom, be it in Lenin Park or in Havana's Cathedral Square.

Her house is almost hidden by trees which are flowering shrubs, sweet basil, roses and violets that grow, beautiful, in an ugly basin. Her small parlor is filled with books and pottery. Two guitars and a violin hang on the wall, close to a music stand with a score on it. The round center table is covered with objects, beside her rickety rocker in which she sits with her guitar and says she's a happy woman.

"I have every reason to be happy," she says with shining eyes and a smile, "because I've produced a body of work and I've taken it to the remotest corners of my country, and because the children know and sing my songs. Besides," she adds with her youthful face, "I'm adding something to the world."

Author of over 200 songs, 50 of them for children, and composer of the music for Gabriela Mistral's *Rondas* (Rounds) and José Martí's *Ismaelillo*, she confesses that she prefers children. "They don't care how old you are, or if you're pretty or ugly or what your dress is like.

Either they like you or they don't and they tell you."

Like a magical toy, her guitar rests on her lap. Without artifice, in a natural position, her fingers strum the strings, produce some notes, the most whimsical, while she continues to explain, with clear and detailed ideas, her complicated minstral career.

Back in Santa Clara, where she was a school teacher, she dreamed of doing what she now does. She arrived in Havana in the 60's and her dream came true at the peña in Lenin Park, where she is something of a Jill-of-all-trades: a teacher, reporter, cultural promoter who calls for audience participation, and above all, a trovador.

"I prefer that to the lights and stage of a theater, which make me feel like a tiny bird in a shoebox," she says with a laugh. "When the distance is filled with pastures and hills, I don't mind it because I figure I'm singing to the mockingbirds and the ceiba trees, the hutias and the lizards, in a word, for everybody. That's the way it is in Lenin Park, at the Peña. I sing and look at the trumpet woods and the road, it's really an indescribable sensation for me.

"Guests at the Peña have been people I greatly admire, like Alicia Alonso, Raquel Revuelta, Ana Lasalle. Artists, researchers, story tellers, poets and artisans, visitors from all over the world who take an interest in a very exciting experience. They tell of their joys and sorrows, the ups and downs of their careers. Communication with the audience is very direct thanks to the natural surroundings, the atmosphere of solidarity helps a great deal to achieve this objective.

"That's why I say," she adds with satisfaction, "that I sing at the Peña as if it were my home, and in fact, it is. The Peña Cathedral Square provides a test for the art of the minstral, an unusual setting with people passing by, going on their way or staying to chat."

Then she says, seated in her rocker and surrounded by her favorite plants and pets, that whenever she sings in an open space, she thinks of the old stories about country towns, trees and birds that her father told her when she was a child. As she sings, anchored to her guitar, she sees horizons.

"THEY ARE MY FUTURE"

"I wouldn't want a better audience than children because they're natural and spontaneous. I also love waterfalls, the sun, cold and rain. I like to fill my songs with all sorts of things as a chronicler of my time and its course. So, sometimes I sing to a basin I found in a rubbish heap, or to a cat,—I have five of them—to *romerillo*, an aromatic herb. My love for children and nature are more decisive for me than books and the influence of poets and musicians. I'm convinced that happiness is more important for me than knowledge and everything else, my own happiness and the happiness of others. I know that good teachers and mothers aren't lacking, but there is a lack of people who know how to talk to children and be understood by them."

A teacher who decided to be guided by her musical vocation over two decades ago, Teresita confirms with some nostalgia that she'd happily go back to teaching, to be able to teach children about the grandeur of the Revolution. But she consoles herself with the fact that she makes children happy with her songs.

After many years of hard work, this genuine creator experiences the joy of hearing her music in big shows like the one presented for International Year of the Child, in plays at the Puppet Theater, in ballet and on television. Also, when she hears people singing her songs, she feels proud because she knows she is useful.

"I attended a huge Pioneer children's activity, and in the silence preceding the words of the speaker, nearly 500 children broke into one of my songs. You can't beat that for emotion. Or the way a little girl, in a school, said to me, with admiration in her eyes: 'Hey, you're so pretty.' And then I burst out laughing, and she asked me, worried, 'Are you happy?' because I laughed so hard I started to cry at the idea that she found me pretty at the age of fifty and with these glasses. After that she came over and touched my guitar and said, 'your guitar is made of gold.' In Cathedral Square something similar happened. A little girl who lives there went down to the Square to comb my hair, and her mother called down from the balcony, to tell her that I'd be angry. The little girl looked at me very seriously and asked me, 'you won't scold me, will you?' Those things don't happen at performances for adults.

"Sometimes I meet grown men who say: 'The last time I saw you I was a little boy.' So I see that twenty years ago I had children who today are my present, while today I have others who are my future. That rejuvenates me and makes me feel useful."

TRIBUTE TO MARTÍ

Despite the severe scoldings by her mother, a piano teacher of considerable prestige in Santa Clara, Teresita could never get through the endless, boring Slava exercises. The piano was out of reach for her, an outsize thing that lorded it over the large front room of the old house and sounded at all hours.

But because the girl loved songs and was interested in both music and poetry, after convincing her mother she'd never become a piano virtuoso, she chose the guitar. Only then she was able to learn to play the instrument with a trovador who was well known to all the roving musicians of the day. "The guitar is everything to me when I compose," she says while rehearsing the most evasive arpeggios. "It is the perfect instrument for the song made of poetry and music, because there is a kind of subtle alloy of voice, words, accompaniment and the way of playing. When you play the piano, as you press a key you have to wait until it reaches the martinet and goes *boing*. With the guitar, your fingers are the martinet, and sometimes you're thinking of a note, a chord, and you're hearing it thanks to what they call inspiration, love, creative sense, sensibility, and at the same time you've got it literally at your fingertips. Besides, the way you hold it means that as you play you feel it close, and that its sounding box is your own. As soon as I concentrate on the poem and hear the music of its words, it drags along the words like a faithful dog.

"For instance, I didn't try to set Martí to music, because he doesn't need any music. What I did was to follow humbly what the words suggested to me, and build a kind of pedestal for the poem. That's why the music to *Ismaelillo* doesn't swallow the poem, instead, Martí prevails. The result isn't a song by Teresita Fernández but Martí's poetry, that's why I'm very pleased with that job."

As she now confesses, when she began the complex work of setting to music Gabriela Mistral's *Rondas* and Martí's *Ismaelillo*, she did not think anyone would be interested. People were used to conventional songs and it was necessary to break that pattern. "But I said to myself," she says emphatically, "I put the music there and let it fly. In any case, someone was working on the text. It was like publicizing a body of work that was much more valuable than my own songs."

Teresita always admired Mistral's having been a country school teacher, and her austerity. "Martí, too, was very austere, and he did his best work in silence. In addition, they created a language in poetry on the basis of the blending of cultures, an original form of expression that continues to prevail in Spanish America.

"If I had to set something else of José Martí to music, it would be *Nuestra América* (Our America). All his writings are important, but this is the one that is closest to our time, and perhaps it would be better able to reach the fraternal peoples of the continent. Of course the whole thing could not be set to music, some fragments would be recited by an actor. When I set *Ismaelillo* to music, it was because I considered its great worth and felt indebted to Martí until I finished it. Now I think that in addition to being recorded for orchestra, arrangements could be made for choirs, opera, ballet, because the images of the poem, as in *Musa traviesa* (Mischievous Muse) have movement, rhythm. Besides it would mean giving greater hierarchy to the work of the Master."

CREATION, A GOLDEN BIRD

Teresita is surprisingly enthusiastic in her conversation. She is dynamic and energetic. She is very expressive, and her words convey her watchful sensibility and her very special way of seizing beauty.

"A while ago I read something that consoled me with my guitar and my little songs. After I read that art began in the caves of Altamira, I felt that humans couldn't possibly come up with anything better. But when I read Isaac Asimov's *The Naked Sun*, because I love science fiction, convinced that I was just an old woman with her guitar and her songs, in some chapter, one of the characters of the novel boasted of possessing an ancient instrument and pulled out a guitar and sang a love song, I felt that I could settle with what I am and what I do. Then, one day a young woman who works with computers said to me, 'I love to come hear you sing, because I rest.' So I guess that despite the development of computers and space ships, the little which I sing to will always be needed."

"If I had to choose the song I like best, I'd say with full conviction that I still haven't composed it. I like best that song which urges me to discover, feel and think. I like composing better than singing because creation is the greatest pleasure there is, it means perpetuating our passage through life."

Teresita is convinced that creation is a golden bird that each creator seizes in their own way. The sculptor uses stone, the musician, notes, the poet, words. The materials vary, but beauty is one. Creating, she says, is comparable only to learning and teaching, because in all three cases, a similar sort of bedazzlement takes place.

"I think that all kinds of work are important," she says convincingly and workers are very deserving of respect. Everything has its science and its art, but the difference between a mediocre worker and a brilliant one in their specialty is the ability to create.

"When I read Máximo Gómez's *Diario de Campaña* (Campaign Diary) or about Maceo and Gómez's sweep across Cuba (in the 1895 independence war) or about the Moncada fortress attack, and I think about the cost of this Revolution, I think that talking about my work, my songs, is quite ridiculous.

"I don't regard myself as a great artist, but I do think I'm a good person, and what matters is having a good opinion of yourself", she says honestly. "I'm a minstrel women with a guitar, and that's it. I'm not vain, for instance, when I'm on a bus or in the street and people look at me, I always figure it's because something's wrong with my clothes, and I start checking from head to toe, until someone say, 'Aren't you the woman who sings to the children?' Then I remember that I'm an artist."

Teresita Fernández at Lenin Park

SURPRISE ENCOUNTER

Teresita's 50th birthday caught her off guard. She realized she really was fifty and that her work was important the day they celebrated it at the Peña in Lenin Park. That afternoon, Marta Valdés sang some of Teresita's songs on love, death, loneliness, leavetakings and meetings. Silvio Rodríguez sang to her his fine *Rabo de nube* (Twister). Cintio Vitier read verses by José Martí, and suddenly, she realized that all those around her loved her.

"With my work something similar happened as with my 50th birthday. One day I looked back and realized I'd written a number of songs including setting *Ismaelillo* to music, my most important work. And since I've been creating all the time, the balance was overwhelming. I suddenly realized that I had produced a great amount of work, and I was surprised. Pleasantly surprised."

THE RUMBA BREAKS OUT

THE cool patio with its laurel trees and bougainvillaeas is still quiet. The hundred or so spectators who surround the large space for dancing wait with keen expectation for the rumba to break out so they can really enjoy themselves.

On a platform to one side, the *tumba*, the *llamador* and the *quinto*, the different-size drums that provide the rhythmic seasoning for the rumba, wait for the percussionists, who begin to caress their skins.

The soloist takes the microphone in his hand and breaks the discrete silence of the listeners with his clear voice, in the introduction of *diana* (literally, reveille). Parallel to the story told by the improviser-soloist with his fine voice, the chorus breaks in with its repetitive phrase and the guaguancó is in full swing.

The couple who move into the center of the dance space launch their sexy game of the *vacunao* (literally, vaccination) or humping, a pelvic movement charged with eroticism. The male brings into play all his skill as a dancer around the female, who, aloof and vain, protects herself from the sensual onslaught with prodigious steps.

The solist's fine voice tells of infidelities and love affairs, and about the alleged death of Malanga, "the greatest rumba man of all," while the dancers pursue their game of surrender and flight, with the rhythm marked by the quinto drum and the woman's gestures as she slides her stole or bandana over her body, thereby further exciting the male or else covers her breasts with her crossed arms.

The story is capped by the woman's "surrender," as she allows herself to be possessed, and then leaves the scene with her man.

The ring of onlookers opens up, and they encourage a new couple to dance. Rumba is in the air; the rhythm is once again a group festivity, just as it was early in the century in the *solares* of Havana and tenement houses in Matanzas. Many families still maintain the old tradition of the rumba.

The rumba, which can be sung, danced and played, takes on new life in the lovely courtyard of the National Folklore Company.

Despite a cold front that makes Havanan'inhabitants wear jackets and sweaters, things are hot in this open space in the Cuban capital because the "rumba broke out."

RUMBA'S CUBAN FEATURES

Rumba used to be a source of fun and release for the enslaved people who were brought to Cuba. It brought joy to the black people living in the city tenements and on the sugar cane plantations.

In time musical elements of Congos, Lucumís or Yorubas and Carabalís joined the original core, which may have been of *Gangá*, West African roots. Hispanic features such as melodic line and model rhymes also became part of the rumba.

According to late Cuban ethnologist and musicologist Argeliers León, the rumba is "a fiesta in which is represented what lingers in one sector of the population of cultural elements that converge through its members, in a situation of profound changes in social relations leading to the breakdown of original functions. It is that which endows the rumba with its profane, that is, non-sacred, nature."[1]

The rumba is not a replica of African ritual dances nor of the Spanish *cuplé*. It is a version of those original elements, a new expression of

[1]Argeliers León, *Del canto y del tiempo* (On Songs and Time), 2d ed., Havana, Ed. Letras Cubanas, 1984, p. 152.

the rejected sectors of colonial and neocolonial society that takes the form of the songs of the guaguancó, something like an accurate chronicle of daily life, and the gestures of the *columbia* dancer, who at times takes up a machete to represent the sugar cane cutter. The columbia sprang up precisely in the heart of intensive plantation agriculture.

If the word rumba is identified with such Afro-American terms as tumba, *tambo*, *macumba*, all of which mean merrymaking group, its practice, which early in the century gave rise to the choruses and musical groups in a number of Havana districts, has ceased to be the exclusive property of a single sector of the population, and is now the purest musical expression of what is Cuban.

THREE CRATES AND A DANCER

From the start, rumba was improvised just about anywhere: in a tenement room or yard, in the street, in the lane between fields of sugar cane. All that was needed was enough space for a ring of onlooker-participants.

The lack of proper drums was no obstacle. People grabbed a board or a drawer, a door, the seat of a rawhide chair, spoons and even the frying pan from the kitchen.

An empty codfish crate re-assembled to suit the tastes of the percusionists provided the bass sound. The small wooden crates used to pack candles nicely imitated the higher sound of the quinto, the drum that engages in a dialogue with the dancer.

The story is told of a *rumbero*, practitioner of rumba, who needed a coach to take him and his voluminous collection of wooden boxes and crates to the site of a rumba party.

One famous rumba group was the Tahona (literally flour mill) from the Carraguao neighborhood of Havana, which took its name from the drums (actually flour crates) it used. Every May 20 and Christmas the members of Tahona performed a street rumba that resembled the conga. Before the dancers passed by, local people decorated the streets with flowers and garlands. Then they rewarded them for their performance of the different steps as the *reseda*, the *giribilla* and the *palatino*, with shared toasts and ribbon rosettes containing coins of that time such as louis d'or and centenes.

In Matanzas, said to be the birthplace of the rumba, the Banço Azul Rumba Society was founded in 1911. Its members were Cuban-born blacks who took up money collections to celebrate their birthdays. The traditional fare was a vast caldron of peppery oxtail and bottomless basins of a brew whose main ingredients were rum and gin. In one corner of the spacious hall where the merrymakers danced, ate and drank was the "seat of punishment," with its plushy cushions and ribbon-hung back. Anyone who sat in it had to pay a fine consisting of buying several bottles of wine or a sucking pig.

STYLES OF RUMBA DANCING

The *yambú*, the guaguancó and the columbia are the most outstanding kinds of rumba. The first two are urban-bred, while the columbia is typically rural.

The yambú is the oldest, and the woman is the star. In the guaguancó, man and woman share the spotlight. The columbia is danced only by men.

The yambú consists of stately, smooth and melodious movements. The woman flirts, while the man takes second place and does not engage in the pelvic movement known as vacunao to pursue his prey. According to old yambú dancers, it goes "all the way to Spanish times." The guaguancó is performed by a couple, a singer and a drummer who plays the quinto, the drum that calls the steps and the choreography.

The exact date of the birth of the guaguancó is unknown, but it quickly took over in Havana. Rival Havana districts, with their choruses, such as Los Roncos from the Pueblo Nuevo district, and El Paso Franco from Pilar, created compositions of marked patriotic, anti-imperialist content. One of the best-loved was a guaguancó by Gonzalo Asencio,

The rumba breaks out

better known as Uncle Tom, given the official repression he was sent to jail for the words of his rumba.

The events of the diry politics of the pseudorepublic period (1902-1959) were chronicled in biting satire or laughing mockery in the guaguancó.

The columbia is for men only, for macho men with fancy footwork and shoulder movements. The player of the quinto drum must be an excellent percussionist to be able to highlight on the skins the dancer's acrobatics with a more segmented playing than the guaguancó beat.

The columbia dancer must respond with gestures that imitate flying a kite, strolling about, playing baseball, cutting cane and even shooting a gun to the expert drummer who beats out many and varied rhythms, while the soloist with his laments or *llorao* fires musical digs or provocations at the dancer that are more exhausting that his own movements.

This afternoon, after the guaguancó, rumba is in the air and the air grows more heated when the columbia begins. The younger men move about restlessly. The first among them steps out and raises a forefinger to ask the onlookers for permission to begin. After the circle of participants opens, the young man salutes the drums, removes his shoes and launches into a display of skill with dazzling pirouettes and juggling a machete.

Then a new dancer takes his place and the heat of the dance rises as he attempts to outdo his predecessor. Finally, the spontaneous participation of the dancers reaches the onlookers so deeply that many of them break into the circle to compete with the sweat-covered rumbero who showed he was the best of them all.

CUBA Internacional. January 1984

THE CHANGÜÍ

JULIA Reyes, the oldest dancer of the Guantánamo changüí wears a red satin gown. She marks the beat with stately delight. Her old face is impassive while her partner, 20 years her junior, twists and turns in energetic parabolas around her, to finish the dance exhausted.

The changüí is played with a handful of instruments: the tres, the same used in traditional country tunes, maracas, a guayo, *bongó* drums and a *marímbula* that provides the base sound. The changüí, a curious rhythm, is more syncopated than the *son*, and is native to Guantánamo, Cuba's easternmost province.

Julia Reyes maintains the peculiar beat of the chorus, and her partner is forced, by the *bongos*, to speed up his footwork. In fact, changüí lore claims that even the oldest woman dancer can run through ten male partners in a session of dancing.

THE *SON* IS A NEW THING

Chicho Ibáñez, an exceptional *son* musician who is now over 100 years old, says that the changüí, characteristic of Guantánamo, is prettier than the *son*. "I like it," he once remarked firmly, "because it was the first thing I improvised on my three-stringer, with the help of

, some lady's hairpins. I still didn't know you were supposed to use your nail to pluck the strings. The *son* is a new thing, anyway."

Every bit as old as Chicho is this item from a newspaper of the day: "There are favorable reports on music on the Island. Suffice it to say that black women are singing in the churches and the güiro now used in the country changüís, appeared among the instruments."

According to Esteban Pichardo, the changüí is "a certain vulgar dance and gathering of hoi, polloi, an Afro-Cuban dance that is synony-mous of *guateque*,"[1] in other words, a gathering of the people, espe-cially black and mulattoes, where there was singing and dancing.

Fernando Ortiz (1881-1969), a profound researcher into the roots of Cuban culture, states in his *Nuevo catauro de cubanismos* (New Collection of Cuban Usage) that "the academic meaning could also come from the Congo verb *sanga*, which means, in addition to dance, to jump with joy and to triumph: *changüí* would then be the manifes-tation of pleasure or joy of the author or the chorus and the word must have been introduced by black slaves in their games with the the white children, the young masters. In its academic meaning the word *changüí* is thought to come from the Spanish gypsy word "changüí" (trick, deception), according to Rebollado. But this does not rule out the possibilty of a black African origin of the Gypsy word, as is the case in the *caló* or popular speech of the Spanish gypsies."[2]

Like the *son oriental*, the changüí appeared in the 19th century in Baracoa and Guantánamo, as demonstrated by the research of com-poser Rafael Inciarte. The exact spot where the changüí came into existence was the Santa Justa farm at El Cobre, not far from Santiago. Data compiled by veteran *son* practitioner Delfino Puente, who is also from Guantánamo, show that back in the 1870's the repertoire of the musical group led by his father included sones that the musi-cians called changüís. Puente remembers that the instruments were a three-stringer, bongo drums, a pair of spoons and a pair of maracas. In addition, everyone took part in the changüí, which is song and dance together.

[1]Esteban Pichardo, *Diccionario provincial cuasi razonado de vozes (sic) y fra-ses cubanas* (Provincial Dictionary of Quasi Itemized Cuban Terms and Phrases), Havana, Editorial de Ciencias Sociales, 1978, p. 209.

[2]Fernando Ortiz, *Nuevo catauro de cubanismos*, Havana, Editorial de Ciencias Sociales, 1975, p. 279.

Changüi

WHO SAYS IT'S NOT FROM GUANTÁNAMO?

Some people say that in another eastern province, Manzanillo, on the south coast, there used to be a musical genre called the *bunga*, also known as the changüi. The instruments included a *quijada*, a jawbone, preferably that of a donkey because of its bigger sound, and the *bunga* or *botijuela*, a clay pot used to import olive oil from Spain. When blown, the botijuela made a base sound.

Notwithstanding its appearance in several areas of Cuba's easternmost region, the changüi is acknowledged to be Guantánamo's typical traditional music. The changüi was present in Guantánamo long before the 1895 Independence War, in the mill yards and slave quarters of the San Miguel sugar estate, near today's Jamaica municipality, and it was played and sung by Atina Latamblé, the precursor, accompanied by his sons Higinio and Vicente.

Reyes Latamblé, director of Guantánamo's most outstanding changüí group, is a descendent of Atina. Latamblé says that his group of five musicians and a dance team, who play at as many as 15 dances a month at *Círculos sociales*, workplaces and schools, maintains the authentic melodic line of this variation on the oriental *son*—although not all sones can be arranged as changüís—which many specialists claim is the root of the legitimate Cuban *son*.

CUBA Internacional. March 1979

"You Have to Move with the Times"

FÉLIX Chapottín became known as a great of the trumpet in the Habanero Sextet when the *conjunto* was "infecting" the capital with the *son*, a new arrival from Oriente, the eastern region.

Since then he's been improvising phrases, polishing unmistakable high notes which during the montuno section of a *son*, provide fine seasoning for the rhythm. He's been doing flourishes on the chorus in his very own Chapottín way for 60 years, and he is fond of saying that he plans to die of old age while making music.

Félix is not conversationalist. He speaks in spurts. When he tells a story, he's delightful, but otherwise, he becomes all nerves and punctuates his words with the movements of his knotty fingers.

He says in a deep, slow voice: "I owe my musical studies to my godfather. He was an extremely sensitive man who realized that I had musical leanings from watching my games as a boy. I have him to thank for what I am. My first instrument wasn't a trumpet, it was a tuba almost as big as I was. I was eleven years old and played in the Children's Band of Guanajay, not far from Havana. I got my first trumpet from members of the Liberal Party to play their song, *La chambelona* (The Lollypop).[1] That was all part of the political scene

---

[1] The name was taken by a group of Liberal Party members that rose up in arms in 1917 against the conservative government. "—Ed."

back then. The Liberals used their catchy tune, *La chambelona*, and the Conservatives had their big congas in the street, and they all tried to distract the people. In any event, we were just as bad off no matter which party won the election. I lived on *La chambelona* for two years, then I got tired and went back to Havana, my home town. Here, someone who'd heard me play remarked: 'that black guy is a wonder on the trumpet,' and one day I got tapped by the Havana Sextet, which was making history with the *son*. I could hardly believe it, but I started with them and I was determined to make good. I always tried to correct the flaws in the Havana Sextet and in the other outfits I played with. The better they played, the more outstanding I became.

"I taught and learned at the same time. Just about every day we played at balls in dance academies and private associations, but I preferred the Sunday dances of the working people in the gardens of the Tropical and Polar breweries. They were really fun because of the popular atmosphere."

"A BIG-MOUTHED REBEL"

Although it remains to be confirmed that the *son* titled *Ma'Teodora* was the very first in history, it really did exist. Despite the rhythmic and melodic variations of the initial version, *Ma'Teodora* prevails as a point of departure and it already displays the defiant nature of the *reginas* or quartets, the rural *son's* forebears.

"No doubts about it, the mulatto man Nené Manfugás was the one who brought the *son* out of the Baracoa mountains and the hills around Guantánamo. One day he grabbed his tres, an instrument that was practically unknown in the city, and took off for the carnival in Santiago. He was the wonder of the day, with his strange sort of guitar to which he sang all kinds of sones. He even dared to sing.

> *Cantador que se dilata*
> *conmigo no forma coro,*
> *si tiene diente de oro,*
> *yo se lo pongo de plata.*

(A singer who takes too long / will never join me in a chorus, / and if he's got a gold tooth, / I'll turn into silver for him.)

"No one dared to respond to that challenge."[2]

Many of those four-line "quartets" warned the Cuban independence fighters, the mambises, of the approach of a Spanish column. The Spaniards found it natural to hear the voice of a mule team driver off in the hills, so they saw nothing amiss when someone sang as they went by:

> Caimán, caimán, caimán,
> ¿adónde está el caimán?
> El caimán está en el paso, mamá,
> y no me deja pasar.

(Alligator, alligator, alligator / where is the alligator? / The alligator's at the pass, Momma, / and he won't let me by.)

So when the "alligators"[3] reached the spot where the mambises had spent the night, all they found were the still-warm ashes of their make-shift cookstove.

"So that's why I say that the *son* was born a rebel," adds Félix Chapottín, nodding his head. "A rebel, a big-mouth you bet. When something went wrong, there was always a *son* about it. That was how we poor musicians got even for the way the thieves and killers that used to run this country kept us hungry. You really need an iron will to blow on the trumpet with an empty stomach. Sometimes things would get all blurry, or I'd even black out. And if that happened to me, with a steady job, you can imagine what other musicians went through. For instance, Chicho Ibáñez had to sell his compositions for under 10 pesos, and he lost his copyright. The thing is, although there were several sextets, the Boloña Sextet, the Occidente Sextet founded by María Teresa Vera, that glory of Cuba, there were lots of *son* musicians and only a few really solid groups. I remember that in the 20's, the three most famous ones were the Habanero Sextet, Ignacio Piñeiro's Sextet and the Matamoros Trio."

---

[2]Musical "controversy" between two improviser singers plays an important role in traditional Cuban music of rural origin. "—T."

[3]It refers to the Spaniards. "—T."

NO *SON* DANCING ALLOWED

In 1909, José Miguel Gómez, the president of the pseudorepublic (1901-1959) who institutionalized the large-scale theft of state funds, issued an order that would take the *son* to all parts of the country, although his intention was clearly not musical. Fearful of frequent uprisings in the army, he ordered the soldiers to be transferred away from their place of origin. The soldiers from Oriente brought the *son* to the capital, while the inhabitants of Havana introduced the guaguancó in Oriente.

In 1920 the Habanero Sextet was founded and four years later it made its first recordings in the United States. The *son*, symbol of Cuban nature, then achieved international renown.

"Sure, the *son* became famous, but it was always close to the poor people, black, brown and white. When poverty worsened after World War II, the *son* underwent a new era of popularity compared with the old typical orchestra and the jazz bands that were so fashionable among the well-to-do. We can thank Arsenio Rodríguez and trumpet player Julio Cuevas, who composed some that were like a slap in the face of the politicians, for that popularity. The groups began to grow with new instruments-the slide trombone, more than one trumpet, the conga drum and later on, electronic keyboards. Now, in my opinion, we have Benny Moré to thank for the popularity of the son montuno. There's no one like Benny Moré. A self-taught musician, he did his arrangements in his own way. He'd call on a musician who knew how it was done, and he'd tell him where the instrument should go. The arranger would then have to write Benny's music, the way he wanted it: after all, he was the director of his Giant Band.

"I remember how Machado's[4] Minister of Interior, Zayas Bazán, banned the *son*," says Chapottín with a somber expression on his face. "We found a spot in the Pocitos sector of Havana, the police did not dare to go there, and we'd dance all night.

[4]Gerardo Machado, president of the pseudorepublic from 1925 to 1933. "—Ed.".

"Sometimes we'd go to the associations of the rich whites, or else we'd go out on their yachts to play for them. The bongó drums were banned too, so we invented our own *pailas* or kettle drums. Only the Habanero Sextet was allowed to use the bongó drum. When Machado fell we came out in the open again. Thanks to the phonograph and records, the North Americans got rich. Music was a big business, and people wanted *son*."

"MIGUELITO CUNÍ WAS THERE"

In 1950, Arsenio Rodríguez, known as the "blind marvel" went to New York. His group included trumpet player Félix Chapottín and singer Miguelito Cuní, who worked together for over 30 years with the *son*. Félix took over the group, which became known as Chapottín and his All Stars, and they brought new life to such popular numbers as *El carbonero* (Charcoal Man), El *quimbombó* (Okra) and La *guarapachanga*.[5] Today, despite his advanced age Chapottín achieves on the trumpet brilliant notes that accompany Miguelito Cuní, "the best of the living soneros," according to his old friend.

"I once said that Chapottín was Cuní and viceversa, because we really form a unit. We met through music and music still unites us. When I joined Arsenio's group, Cuní was there, and he handed over the position of director to me, because his personality wasn't the most suited for that, as he told me. We managed, even in bad times. When the cha-cha-chá appeared, we incorporated it into the *son*, and we kept on with other contributions, without giving up our usual, strictly Cuban music. You have to flow with the times, otherwise the public turns away to follow the latest craze. I remember how we'd get together in the food store at Zanja and Chávez streets, waiting anxiously for a phone call to tell us we'd got some gig. Back then there

[5]*Guarapo* means sugar cane juice, the *pachanga* is a noisy festivity that would later give its name to a dance. "—T."

were no contracts or regular pay, you'd get 50 or 60 pesos for playing all night, and that was it. What it meant was having to split up the
money among all the musicians in the band, in a word, we shared our
poverty. Anyhow, we trovadores and soneros had fun in our own
way. We'd find our material all over-the neighborhood charcoal vendor, the eviction of poor people who could not pay their rent. What a
difference today, with the *son* travelign along all roads and telling
about such inspiring things! That's why I feel so great, stronger than
ever. I'm coming to realize, with this interview, that you can get a
whole life into a handful of words. Also, that I have to live fast to get
the most out of the years to come."

GENTLEMAN OF THE *SON*

T HIS tall man with the stately demeanor and the faultless suit is a very special singer of the *son*. He barely moves on the stage. Only his strong, mellow sonero's voice takes off and takes hold in the hall.

He does move his long hands at exactly the right moment of the chorus, to stress the story. He sustains the high note that blends into the air like a birdsong.

He never turns toward the band and he never dances. What he does is improvise, this master of the montuno. His clean, whole voice mounts threefold over the filligree woven by the trumpet with brief phrases of the song's moral set to verse.

He seems to come from the bottom of time, from forever, as he presents the best and deepest of the incredible Cuban *son*.

Serious, confident. Miguelito Cuní is like that, and that is the way he sings, this gentleman of the lasting *son*.

FESTIVAL OF SONEROS

Guantánamo was all *son* for the three-day National Festival. It was sung in peñas and theaters, parks and plazas. Soneros from all over

Cuba met in Guantánamo, the first town to citify the country-born rhythm. They were all there, performers and musicologists, and in their presentations they sought to unravel the course of this song whose chorus is like a hymn of the people.

A formidable all-star orchestra was organized under the name of *Homenaje* (Homage) to pay tribute to two veteran soneros, Félix Chapottín and Miguelito Cuní.

The Festival was dedicated to them and their half century of *son*. But nothing was said about the tribute until the plane carrying the Chapottín orchestra and other musicians landed at Guantánamo. It was supposed to be a surpirse, and it was.

"I just had to cry when I found myself in the midst of lots of people greeting us with banners and flowers. Sure, I had to cry, because as soon as Chapottín and I appeared in the doorway of the plane, a band began to play. Pioneer kids surrounded us down on the tarmac and one of them read a statement of welcome. So I found out that the *Son* Festival was dedicated to Chapottín and me. I was really surprised by the tribute. It just never occurred to me that I was important. All of a sudden I felt really happy, and kind of light, as I'd taken a load off my shoulders. I greeted everyone, as shy as a kid. Like a kid who's just graduated as a sonero."

CUNÍS'S ABC

"A good sonero," says Miguelito Cuní, "must know how to sing the bolero, guaracha, rumba and guaguancó. He has to adapt his voice to each rhythm to give it the proper timbre. Above all, he has to know how to improvise, that's very important.

"For instance, I find that listening to classical music is basic. It tunes my ear, especially opera. I feel that I learn how to place my voice by listening to the great tenors and baritones. My favorite composer is Tchaikovsky.

"I knew some very good soneros: Cheo Marquetti, Arsenio Rodríguez, Abelardo Barroso. They set the rules for the *son*. We used to call

Barroso *el Decano* (the Dean). Everything that Benny Moré did (now, there's no one like him), everything I do, it all springs from Barroso."

With the permission of his older sister, the head of the household, Miguelito Cuní went out to sing at the age of fourteen.

And with the fascinated curiosity of the adolescent, he began to discover the world of music.

Then he lived in Pinar del Río, in the midst of a large family, and he dreamed of studying medicine. That is, until he peered into the café at Retiro and Rosario streets, where the trovadores met, and fell in love with so many guitars and songs. He began to test the potential of his baritone's voice. He became popular as a mascot of the old timers, until he joined Niño Rivera's Sextet. In 1938 he arrived in Havana, contracted by Ernesto Muñoz, and a few days later made his debut on Radio Progreso as a singer with the Muñoz Band.

"My voice was thicker then. But since you have to sing the *son* high, improvise with a loud voice to shine in the montuno, it's gotten thinner on me with the years."

The boleros and sones that he sang were arranged by Muñoz and international numbers by Rafael Fernández, Pedro Flores, Agustín Lara. "No one should get jealous over what I'm about to say, but my favorite composer has always been the Mexican Agustín Lara. His sones are very fine. My favorite of the younger soneros is Pablito Milanés. Many of his *sones* will be the sones of the future, thanks to his contributions. Maybe people don't appreciate that now, but music is like a time bomb in a cave. It goes off now, and after a while the sound comes back."

I RESPECT MY AUDIENCE

"Let me tell you a story that shows how I respect my audience. A few years ago I went to Varadero to perform with the Chapottín group. The winter was cold that year, and in the place where we were playing, we got blasts of cold air from the sea. Our only audience was a single table. The rest of the cabaret was empty and we all wondered when they'd leave. Out of respect for them, I sang well, better than ever. After a while the lights went on and the people from the table came up to say hello to me. They were none other than Joan Manuel Serrat and his group, and they were there precisely to hear me sing."

Since 1950 Félix Chapottín, trumpet and director of the group, and Cuní, its singer since it was directed by the late Arsenio Rodríguez, have been inseparable.

"Arsenio introduced the conga drum in the son. It's thanks to him that in 1938 favorable changes in the instrumentation of the son came about. He was a great player of the three-string guitar, he was an honor to Cuba and when he died, in the United States, they had to take up a collection to bury him.

"I knew there was a Chapottín around who played trumpet with the Habanero Sextet, and one day I saw him in my home town. We struck up a friendship. Years later we played together in the group and we've been like one ever since.

"Chapottín is another one who created a style. In my opinion he's a wonder on the trumpet. He knows how to phrase the montunos better than anyone else."

TIME, THAT FRIEND

Miguelito Cuní is a charming, witty man. He loves to tell a good story and let it settle while he falls silent and meditates. He celebrated his 60th birthday and confessed that now, at his age, what he likes best is to sing for his family, or at a friend's house for a handful of people. He is a natural and humble man.

He prefers not to talk about the poverty, sorrow and overwork of his first decades in Havana.

"That would be like sticking my hand into a dusty old trunk," he says, with a sly smile. "Settle for this: I've sung the son with three-string guitars, regular guitars, orchestra and even a military band, the one in Pinar del Río. I lived the Bohemian life and I knew the greats of the trova, Sindo Garay, Manuel Corona, Alberto Villalón. I have my own sones. To paraphrase one of Sindo's numbers, I've got such a bunch of stories rattling around together that they just can't kill me.

"Let me tell you something: a man's best friend is the time he lives in. And that time will be the way he adjusts to it. We should make our plans as if we were going to die tomorrow or live for another 30 years. Fortunately, I feel as if I were born with this Revolution. Time goes by, but I keep being born again with my sones."

MASTER OF MASTERS

That's what Pablo Milanés calls Miguelito Cuní. The well known composer and singer adds that meeting Cuní, singing with him, becoming his friend, was the coming true of a dream he'd had since he was seven.

"Cuní sang the best-known sones on the jukebox in my neighborhood. That was how I began to admire him as the greatest sonero. Just a year ago we sang together for the first time," says Milanés, who has opened up new paths in the traditional song. "Together we recorded Convergencia (Convergence), which he popularized back in the 50's. and with which I won the prize for the best interpretation awarded by EGREM, the Cuban recording company.

"If, as Cuní says, I'm an exceptional sonero, and if, as he claims, some of my compositions will contribute something to the son in the years to come, I owe it to the great soneros like him who taught me to love the best, most authentic of our popular music."

A Master of the Nueva Trova

P ABLO Milanés' house is quiet except for a faroff car horn and the voice of Haydée, his youngest child. The house is as silent as this taciturn man of medium height who moves around anxiously until he finally settles down at the round bare dining room table.

At first, his sharp gaze, his low, measured voice reflect distraction, as if he were being distracted from meditation. After a few questions about his career overcome his resistance, he takes the initiative in the conversation.

In his 24 years as a musician, he is satisfied about two fundamental experiences: first, as a member of the "feeling" movement and later as one of the founders of the Nueva Trova Movement. Those stages include his experiences as a founding member of the Experimental Sound Group of the Cuban Institute for the Film Art and Industry (ICAIC), and in general, as a representative of the new culture promoted by the Cuban Revolution.

"When you're forty you no longer remember as a surprise or because you decide to remember: you do it with a heartfelt sense of obligation. All the years, the places, the people flow into the inexhaustible stream of life."

That milestone age finds him with a large body of work accomplished and another that is rightly outlining novel means of Cuban, Latin American and Caribbean musical expression.

As a composer and singer he has worked in a very broad range of genres that have the *son* and the guajira as their common roots. And as a trovador that he is, that is, a teller of tales, love, life, combat and death are themes that he handles with stylistic sobriety and high emotional voltage.

THE QUEST FOR THE *SON*

"The day my guitar teacher told me that learning the *son* was somewhat heretical, that I should study the classics, I stopped going to class and set out to find the old soneros and trovadores who used to hang out in the cafés and bars. That's how I learned to make popular music, the music I like."

"I think my form of expression, the way I create are heavily influenced by the *son*. Since I was a kid, out in Bayamo, where I was born, I went to lots of dances where the Eastern Organ played. Later, after I was seven, after we were living in Havana, I used to listen to Miguelito Cuní, the great sonero I always admired and who is now my friend, on the jukebox on the corner."

Tú, mi desengaño (You, my disillusion) was Pablo Milanés'first song. At that time, 1962, "feeling" was very popular and the young songwriter was like a younger brother for the "feeling" musicians and singers.

"Although at first I was greatly influenced by "feeling" as a singer, my first song has certain harmonic and melodic sequences that don't belong to the "feeling line". In 1965, with the *guajira-son Mis veintidós años* (At the age of twenty two) not only did I make a complete break with "feeling" but with myself as well. I began to work on the *son* with that song of mine as my point of departure. Shortly afterwards I joined with other young songwriters in the Center for the Protest Song, founded by the Casa de las Américas. That was where the most representative people of the Nueva Trova Movement first got together."

POETRY FROM DAILY LIFE

Pablo Milanés is a man of rigorous habits as a composer. The author of over 200 songs in different genres, composer of music for much of José Martí's poetry, poems by Nicolás Guillén, Mario Benedetti and César Vallejo, and over a score of Cuban documentaries and films, he explains that he works in different ways. At times, the music comes before the text, or vice versa, and on occasion he writes a song "to order."

"But the music I enjoy most," he says with conviction, "is the music that comes to me from inspiration. I believe in those fecund ideas that we first sense and which then crowd in on us to dictate a poem or a song, with not only poetry and music, but harmony, beat, melody.

"I've often said that the Nueva Trova movement's greatest contribution consists of having promoted the new song from the political and aesthetic standpoint, on the basis of study and research into the roots of our popular music. The old trovadores, without a regular income and doomed to a destructive existence of wandering and poverty, never had such an opportunity. Our development has been possible thanks to government backing. That helps us to express the experiences of the Revolution in a purer language whose poetry comes from everyday life."

EXPRESS IN A NEW LANGUAGE

Endowed with a highly melodious baritone voice, Pablo Milanés has never taken singing lessons. He says that his long experience in singing, since 1959 as a professional, in quartets, trios, duets, accompanied by piano or guitar, and in a typical orchestra, have provided him with "some vocal experience."

When Haydée Santamaría, the late revolutionary fighter who headed the Casa de las Américas, asked him to set a number of poems by José Martí to music in just two weeks, he felt that he was discovering a world. The inner music of those poems emerged in a spontaneous flow, and they were recorded in such a short time.

Pablo Milanés

"That's the loveliest record I've ever made," he stresses. "After that I really got into setting poetry to music. I think sometimes you find in a poem the language you haven't been able to find yourself. I think I'm closer to Martí's poetry than any other, although the poetry of the street also reaches me, the poetry that underlies the way ordinary people talk. I'm always observing human behavior, and I especially love the popular background. These things are conveyed in my songs."

LIKE AN OLD FRIEND

His close communication with the people is summed up neatly by Pablo himself when he says that they greet him like an old friend. He feels that when sentiment and an assessment of reality are joined in a song, the composer grows closer to his audience.

"I think that one of the ways I establish communication with the audience is through the spontaneity of my renditions. I never sing a number the same way. I study it and in a general way, I know how the message is going to work. I think high standards in building a repertoire are very important. And, even though what I most admire in a performer is professionalism and a respectful attitude toward the public—naturally talent is basic—I realize that strict adherence to the technical aspect often destroys sentiment."

Three prestigious musicians have been accompanying Pablo for years: Emiliano Salvador, keyboard, Eduardo Ramos, bass and Frank Bejerano, battery. They understand each other to such an extent that today, Milanés writes songs only for the group.

Pablo is often described as the link between two generations of musicians who admire him for his artistic mastery, his identification with the Cuban *son*, which he rates as his ideal means of expression.

He confesses with a vast smile that erases the serious look from his broad face that, aside from the natural coincidences in his own life that have favored his identification with the *son*, it is the most forcefully Cuban music of all.

"That's why I love and revere it so much. And that's why it makes me very proud when Miguelito Cuní calls me an exceptional sonero and records with me *Convergencia*, a *son* that's close to half a century old."

TRIBUTE TO THE SON

T HE *son* burst on the musical scene in the 20's with the Habanero Sextet. Shortly after Rosillo and Parlá, the forerunners of Cuban aviation, ventured over the Atlantic and the first automobiles maneuvered around the narrow streets of Old Havana, the *son* was quickly becoming the most popular Cuban rhythm.

The inhabitants of Havana were still dazzled by neon signs, the cinema halls where silent images bobbed across the screen, and the radio, when the first records by RCA Victor and Columbia arrived from the United States, to carry the *son* throughout all Cuba, and the entire world.

A *son* sextet consisted of a tres, claves (rhythm sticks), maracas, bongó drums and bass, and they abounded at the end of the 20's.

In 1927 the Ignacio Piñeiro National Septet was founded, with the trumpet as its seventh instrument.

The Septet is the only *son* group from that period that still exists. Thanks to its members, experienced musicians who know and love the rhythm and the repertoire of the late Ignacio Piñeiro, its top figure, the old *son* tradition is keeping alive with the same trust.

AS CUBAN AS THE NATIONAL ANTHEM

They say that in the old days, singing a *son* had a solemn revolutionary connotation. The *son* was born in the mountains of Guantánamo and Baracoa, in eastern Cuba, and it sang out for freedom in the 1895 Independence War. When the war was over, it was the favorite patriotic music of the soldiers of the Army of Liberation who had recently come down from the hills.

After the Habanero Sextet popularized the *son* as an avalanche, it uprooted foreign pop music. At the time the habitués of elegant ballrooms danced to the foxtrot, and the charleston, as jazz bands seemed to be colonizing Cuban popular music. The musicians of the jazz bands, who were mainly blacks and mulattoes, were men of humble trades who were victims of discrimination in all areas. When they began to play the *son*, they did not realize, because of their limited musician instruction, that they were popularizing a wonder that would win a place for itself at the pinnacle of society.

"Yes, at first the *son* was played in secluded places. Because it was so great, rich people had it played at their most intimate parties," says Rafael Ortiz, today the director of the Ignacio Piñeiro Nacional Septet. "That is, until one of them got the idea of hiring the Habanero Sextet to play at the Miramar Yacht Club. They got up phrases for the occasion, and they were placed on a bandstand beside the sea. When the grand ladies saw those six black guys tuning their instruments they had a fit, but when the Sextet broke into a montuno it went straight to their feet and not a couple was left seated. That day the *son* broke the class and race barriers. I'd say the *son* became universal.

"We'd get the lyrics from just about anything: the neighborhood charcoal vendor, the roast turkey that we hardly ever ate at Christmas, the government official who was stealing the people's money. We turned everything into sones.

"With the Revolution," adds Ortiz, "the *son* has reverted to the people completely, and even the young people love it and dance it with pride. They're absolutely right, because only the National Anthem is more Cuban than the *son*."

HAPPY ANNIVERSARY

The Ignacio Piñeiro National Septet is marking its 55th Anniversary. One of its youngest members, is singer Carlos Embale, fifty-eight, and the oldest is Lázaro Herrera, eighty, the outlift's only trumpeter in its long history.

"When I joined Piñeiro's group in 1927, it became a septet," Lázaro says proudly. "Maybe because the son is so Cuban, I prefer to play it than all the other rhythms. I learned to play trumpet when I was sixteen and between then and now I've played all kinds of music, including opera and concert music. I've even played with the National Symphony Orchestra.

"Let me tell you that Ignacio Piñeiro has no match either as a person or as a songwriter," he says solemnly. "As a composer he had the honor of making the Cuban son advance a hundred years. Before Ignacio, the son was just a chorus. He added the opening section, what we call the lyric section. Besides that, the choruses Ignacio wrote for his compositions are different, in keeping with that first section."

The qualities of a good sonero such as love for the son, a great sense of rhythm and complete mastery of their instrument are to be found in Lázaro Herrera, trumpet; Rafael Ortiz, director, guitarist and composer; Rogelio Castellanos, bongo player; Charles Burke, bass; Florencio Hernández, maracas and singer; Israel González, tres; Orlando Bolaños, clave and "second" voice; and Carlos Embale, "first" voice and güiro.

They say that the basic instrument is the tres, the right hand of the piano in the son, while the guitar is the left hand. Those two instruments, seasoned with the distinct beat of the bongós, the rhythmic maracas and the claves need only a great voice, like Carlos Embale's which brilliantly covers all registers. When those elements meet up with a fine tune, the product is a great son.

THAT POET OF THE *SON*

According to Rafael Ortiz, Ignacio Piñeiro was the most sought-after composer of his time because his sones were among the most profound. Both the music and lyrics of his sones were carefully crafted. Yet, he created a number in a few minutes, and what sones he created! They are still among the best.

The Septet's first foreign tour was to the United States, where they recorded for several companies. Shortly afterwards they were hired to play at the Cuban exposition in Seville. There is an anecdote that in Spain, which they toured from one end to the other, they were awarded a prize. As they were celebrating, a priest who had a nearby hotel room, furiously demanded that they stop playing because their annoying music was keeping him awake. But he did accept a drink from the Cubans, then he listened to a couple of sones, and according to those in the know, spent the rest of the night dancing with the Septet.

"Before Ignacio Piñeiro founded the Septet," says Ortiz, "he directed Los Roncos, the biggest guaguancó chorus in Cuban history. There were a number of factors that enabled him to gain a thorough knowledge of our music of African roots. First of all he was born in a *solar* and he knew the songs and dances of the African people belonging to the ethnic associations. Secondly, he worked as assistant to a slave woman who sold *mondongo*, those spicy innards of beef. He was a fine mason, and thanks to his skill in the trade, during the Machado administration he was assigned to lay the luxurious floor of the National Capitol building. But above all he was a poet of the *son*, because he knew thoroughly the songs of the clave, the yambú and the *tahona* predecessors and components of the rumba; the guaracha and the *son*. He also recorded Abakuá and he was a fine rumba dancer. But when it comes to the *son*, he has no match. Nor will there be any match for his verse about the *son*:

> *El son es lo más sublime para el alma divertir,*
> *se debía de morir quien por bueno no lo estime.*

(The *son* is the most sublime thing to please the soul, / and those who fail to appreciate it may as well die.)

The Ignacio Piñeiro National Septet

There is no expression of a kind of Cuban popular music that is more authentic than the *son*, especially the work of Ignacio Piñeiro, which is maintained by his Septet. The *son* has always stood as shock troops against the foreign tendencies aimed at distorting the Cuban origin of many rhythms. Even today it continues playing that social function.

The members of the Septet were awarded Cuba's highest cultural decoration, the Félix Varela Order in the First Degree, which is conferred by the Cuban State upon those who uphold, enrich and reaffirm with their work the combative, internationalist and progressive character of the Cuban cultural movement.

With the victory of the Revolution, the way of life of the members of the Septet radically changed. They no longer had to live in poverty, play at night for a pittance and wake up day after day without steady work. They all joined in the new and different stage, and they had little free time to play at cane cutters' camps, schools, factories. And

105

because successors were needed, the enthusiastic efforts of the veteran soneros led to the formation of the Sierra Maestra group, comprised of recent university graduates who adore the son.

A voluminous picture album of the Septet's rehearsal hall, on Belascoaín Street in Havana, displays evidence of the long careers of the eldest among them. They have transmitted over 300 sones that conserve the most genuine Cuban roots.

It might be thought that a group comprised mostly of people who are almost all in their 70's have become frozen in time and that the fresh salsita or Cuban flavor, demanded in Ignacio's most popular son 'Echale salsita (Put on salsita) hasn't been around for a long time. But the best way for them to show that this is not the case is by pointing to the many medals and awards they have received for their untiring work in the many places where the people asked for their performance and the love of the audiences who regard the Septet with national pride.

Perhaps what keeps its members alive, is the old tradition of beginning its programs with a son by Ignacio Piñeiro, the absolute master who they all revere, and whom they had succedded in representing with dignity and decorum.

Ñico Saquito's Roguish Guarachas

THE swinging doors of the Bodeguita del Medio restaurant open onto a very criollo scene: the Cuban *mojito*, that cocktail seasoned with mint leaves, the congrí and the pork that is roasted in sight of the diners, all served up on bare, battered tables surrounded by rawhide taburetes. Also very criolla is the guaracha sung by late Ñico Saquito, an old man in a starched white guayabera shirt who moved around the Bodeguita's small space as if he were in his own home.

Seated opposite a shelf full of incredible objects deposited by regular or one shot visitors, Ñico Saquito sang in his roguish voice his *Compay gallo* (Buddy Rooster), famous since 1936. Under a map of Cuba plastered with pictures of movie stars, writers, music and political figures, Ñico came up with some little known stories about Cuban traditional music. With his back to a wall that is covered with signatures, pictures and poems dating from the 40's up to the present, the author of over 300 guarachas chatted with a Bodeguita regular about the double meanings in his *María Cristina* or *Chencha la Gambá* (Bowlegged Chencha).

"My songs come from an old saying, a story I hear somewhere or other, a joke, and naturally from the joys and troubles I've experienced in my life. But every one of them has popular roots," he said, sipping a mojito that was prepared especially the way he liked it. Then he perched on his own special stool at the noisy bar to talk, with lucidity that is not easy to find in an 80-year-old, about his captivating, hazardous life.

For over 60 years Benito Antonio Fernández Ortiz answered to the name of Ñico Saquito. *"Saquito* (bag) came from my days as a baseball player. I was a real sack when it came to catching balls, that's what my team mates on the outfit where I played for a few pesos said about me. Then, as a musician, the catchy nickname worked out fine."

ÑICO'S SANTIAGO

Ñico Saquito was born on January 17, 1902 in the Santiago's Tivolí district renowned for its roving musicians. Santiago in those days was a city of palm-lined streets where the sun was attenuated by the interwoven leaves. A city where there were still houses made of woven reed to escape from the frequent earthquakes, poorly lighted streets leading to the sea or the high, thick forests surrounding the town, with its small walled squares, and the old custom of going to the Cathedral after siesta to listen to the choir of clerics singing Christmas carols by the notable 18th century musician Esteban Salas.

Ñico was one of the Santiago kids who used to fly kites from the highest spots in town, one of the youths who after they wore long pants, took off in groups to play their guitars at parties where people drank sangaree and ate roast pork with tiny pastries of *catibía*. A young man skilled in serenades and romantic affairs who loved to see a woman wearing a new dress peering, with discreet impatience, through the windows of thick beams.

Only the precarious economic situation of his family, burdened with numerous children, forced him to leave school and take up the trade of foundryman.

"I think my experiences going from one sugar mill to another to work, having friends all over and seeing so much gave me a taste for the guaracha," he says as he moves out to his small, sunny patio. "I used to get together at serenades and birthday parties with Sindo, Villalón, Figarola and Banderas, great Santiago trovadores who influenced me.

Another one who shared my musical obsession was Siro Rodríguez, when he and I were both mechanic's apprentices. Years later he became famous with the Matamoros Trio. Around that period I somehow managed to find time to write songs. I learned how from a cousin of mine who was an outstanding composer. I never studied music, I compose and sing in my own way, and since I began I've been successful, so that the comparsa Carabalí assigned me to write their songs for the Carnival. Whenever I'd come up with a new song on my guitar, I'd head for Virgilio's, the musicians corner, to sing it for the others, and they'd always like it. Music back then was a hobby for me, but later on, music became, along with baseball, one more way to make a living. That was in the 30's, when almost all the mills shut down because of Machado's harvest restriction. All those months out of work led me to make the rounds of the cafés and restaurants with my guitar. Since I'm a funny guy, and the jokes popped right out, I started to compose guarachas that made people laugh, and in return, they'd give me five or 10 pesos. So I said to myself, Nico, this is better than being a mechanic, better that selling odds and ends, and mangoes, better than bathing horses, because I did all of that to earn some money. I chose music."

GUARACHERO, BUT HONEST

There are different accounts of the origin of the word guaracha. Some specialists say it is of Andalusian origin, others claim it is Amerindian. Spain's Royal Academy of the Language defined it as a "Spanish dance similar to the zapateado" while the term was also applied to a small music grouping whose central instrument was an accordion accompanied by a chorus. Reportedly the accordion was first used in Cuba at the time of the 1868 Independence War, in the central town of Sancti Spíritus. As the instrument spread, the guaracha went with it.

Invariably this type of Cuban popular music from the start spoke satirically of happenings in towns and cities, poking fun at events and customs. Although the alternating of soloist and chorus later disappeared, the chorus was retained to highlight the anecdote. Later on,

109

with the accompaniment of the tres and the guitar, the guaracha adopted a livelier tempo. A new air separated it from the romantic love song to turn it into an expression whose roguishness came to predominate in the 19th century, in the vernacular theater.

At the time the term *guarachero* was used to describe a cheerful, fun-loving type, and also a liar.

"Now, on that score, I assure you, that's not true, at least in my case," said Ñico who suddenly looked serious. "I've never sung anything that's not true. Well, sure, sometimes I do go a bit far and say things I imagine, but they always have a basis in fact. For instance, *Compay gallo* sprang from a story I heard at a wake. Later Antonio María Romeu popularized it in one of his famous danzones, so the story I was told by a sleepless mourner achieved world-wide fame.

"*El jaleo* (The noisy party), *La negra Leonor* (Black Leonor), *No dejes camino por vereda* (Don't go from bad to worse) and *María Cristina* are all the product of that way I have of commenting on what's going on. There's no vulgarity in a single one of my guarachas, that's something I can't stand in a poem or a song.

"The one that says *María Cristina me quiere gobernar / y yo le sigo, le sigo la corriente* (María Cristina wants to run my life / and I act like I go along with her), I wrote it when I got sick of the way a woman tried to order me around. She tried to follow me all over, she watched me like a cop, and since I'm a musician, I certainly couldn't let her go along with me. So we fell out, and that's how I came to write the song that made me famous in many places.

"Then, around 1948, I went to Venezuela to perform for a month and stayed for 10 years. I worked there with a group of Cubans to raise funds for the July 26 Movement. I went to jail and got deported. Since I came back to Cuba after the victory of the Revolution, I've devoted myself to music."

THE SONG AS A DENUNCIATION

The guaracha, a form of Cuba's special brand of humor, became popular back in colonial times. It was forbidden in the press of the time because of the critical tone it adopted toward the oppressive policies of the Spanish government. An article published in the paper *El Regañón de La Habana* (The Havana Scold) on January 20, 1801, expressed anger at the "freedom with which people sing in these streets and in many homes a bunch of songs that stand as an outrage to innocence, an offense to morality... How could anyone care to hear *La morena* (Dark Woman) sing? And what about *La guabina*, which in the mouths of those who sing it, tastes like all the dirty and indecent things imaginable?" Yet, there could hardly be anything more innocuous than *La guabina* that goes like this:

> *La mulata Celestina*
> *le ha cogido miedo al mar,*
> *porque una vez fue a nadar*
> *y le mordió una guabina.*

(Celestina got scared in the sea / cause one time she went swimming / and got bitten by a guabina fish).

"The chorus went like this in Spanish:

> *Entra, entra, guabina,*
> *por la puerta de la cocina.*

(Come, guabina, come / through the kitchen door.)

"My guarachas also criticized the previous (pre-Revolution) system," said Ñico as he plucked at the shiny guitar that went everywhere with him. "I came to Havana in 1930 and made my debut with my quartet on Radio Progreso. I worked in the Martí Theater and the Montmartre Cabaret, and then I founded the Guaracheros de Oriente Quintet. We recorded for Victor and toured Mexico, United States and Venezuela. I never had any problems with my songs until one day a chief of radio ethics suspended *La columbina*, because it denounced the exploitation of the Cuban farmers. Then there was *Al vaivén de mi carreta* (As my Wagon Rolls Along), a guajira that mentions Yankee exploitation in our land, and I couldn't play it until Machado fell (1933). The fact of the matter is that they wouldn't let any of my songs go out over the air, because they were regarded as subversive. They weren't too far wrong, because behind the funny story was a jab at the government."

Then Ñico Saquito left the Bodeguita, that informal autochthonous museum, and emerged on Empedrado, the cobble-stone street that

111

Benito Antonio Fernández Ortiz answered to the name of Ñico Saquito

leads to Cathedral Square. In his left hand he held his guitar and smiled at local residents, who greeted him like a beloved old friend. They were used to his daily presence in the narrow streets of the Old City, and a few of them hum the chorus of one of his guarachas as he passed by. One or another impromptu trovador joins his voice to that of the colorful old man who was happy only when he sang to his people.

THE DANZÓN THROUGH TIME

"IN keeping with a resolution adopted by the National Institute for Musical Folklore Research to pay tribute to Miguel Faílde, creator of the danzón, Cuba's national dance, and to mark the 75th anniversary of the presentation of *Las Alturas de Simpson* (Simpson Heights) on the night of August 12, 1879 in the city of Matanzas, all Cuban composers (present and absent) are invited to send their danzones to the First National Danzón Contest.

"... the entries should follow the traditional pattern of this typical Cuban form: an introduction of eight beats repeated for a total of 16; a trio or violin part, with 32 beats and a final part with a minimum of 32 beats.... The danzones must be fully arranged instrumentally. Composers are free to choose one of the two traditional types of orchestra, the 'typical Cuban' or the *charanga*."[1]

A POPULAR DANCE

According to the newspaper article that argued over the danzón at the end of the 19th century, at all the "dancing schools" in Matanzas

[1] Announcement published in the Cuban papers in 1954 on the occasion of the 75th Anniversary of the Danzón. "—Ed."

the custom was for an orchestra to play with a musician-composer who masterly played the bugle in a danza that was so long that it came to be known as danzón or big *danza*. The composer and artist, Miguel Faílde, was a big favorite of the young generation, was a mulatto tailor, a serious, respectable man, a fine-looking man, who somewhat resembled the eminent musician José White. Faílde played his lovely danzones with his renowned orchestra, and all who heard him were captivated by the strong, deafening sound of the bugle which he played with such gusto and mastery that his eyes looked like they would pop out of his head. And so, the delirious, delighted dancers danced throughout the night in the Lyceum[2] of Matanzas.

The first danzón, *Alturas de Simpson*, was first played in the Lyceum of Matanzas. One night, the most experienced dancers incorporated into the sets of minuet, quadrilles and contredances, complicated figures decorated with colored ribbons and flower arches.

Since its beginnings, and especially with the outbreak of the 1895 Independence War, the danzón came under heavy fire from conservatives and reactionaries. As an element that defined Cuban nationhood, the danzón took root alongside the insurrectional struggle. Biting criticism of the colonial regime was sung in its choruses.

Miguel Faílde played his last danzón in 1920. At the time he gave an account of the origins of the very Cuban dance he created: "It was here in Matanzas where nearly 40 years ago the danzón, under my conduction, was played and danced for the first time. After that I myself took it to Havana and played it. People danced the danzón for the first time in Havana at a family gathering where one of the guests was the famous music teacher Raimundo Valenzuela, who applauded it and accepted it as a typically Cuban dance."[3]

[2]Most Cuban cities and towns in the late colonial and pre-Revolutionary periods had private social clubs called the Lyceum and the Spanish Casino, respectively for middle class mulattoes and whites. In recent years, their premises have become Houses of Culture or community centers open to all. "—T."

[3]Osvaldo del Castillo, *Miguel Faílde, creador del danzón*, Havana, Ed. CNC, 1964, p. 101.

115

At a National Danzón Contest

Nearly a century after *Alturas de Simpson*, the danzón continues to be popular, but it is no longer danced with complicated, minuet-like figures. The evolution of Cuban society has brought about changes in the danzón, which is played by Antonio María Romeu orchestra and sung today by Barbarito Diez. Today's dancers largely ignore the traditional way of dancing the danzón with pauses at certain points in the music, during which couples stood flirting, chatting and fanning themselves.[4]

CUBA Internacional, October 1976

[4]It is still a popular dance in Mexico. "—Ed."

THE *SUCU-SUCU*

WITH his body erect, his shoulders and hips still and a leg movement that marks the beat with mounting impetus, Pelayo dances the *sucu-sucu*.

He likes to let himself be led by the beat of the machete scraping a stone, although the others follow the *bongó*, the *tres*, the *marímbula*, the *claves* and the *maracas*, the same instruments used in the *son*.

The sucu-sucu uses the rhythmic, instrumental and melodic formula of the *son*, and like the *son*, a soloist-improviser and a chorus alternate in the lyrics. That accounts for its resemblance to the *changüí*, the Cayman Island round dance, the Jamaican calypso, the Puerto Rican *plena*, the Colombian *porro* and the Haitian-Dominican *merengue*, all examples of the influence of the *son* in the Caribbean that subsequently evolved according to their region of origin.

Pelayo, a giant of a man with a thin old face, remembers what sucu-sucu fiestas were like in his youth. Women wore ankle length cotton gowns with ruffles and ribbons, while the men wore white guayabera shirts and straw hats. Usually these community gatherings took place under a palm thatched roof with a ring of taburetes and benches around a dance floor where people danced the night away.

"I won lots of prizes in dance contests in Gerona, La Ceiba and La Fe, the biggest towns on Isle of Pines," he says with a look of pride. There was nobody who could come near Pelayo when it came to moving his legs without losing the beat, "that's what my *compañero*

Mongo used to say when I danced, and I ended up believing him. I also remember how I made my first guitar: I took a piece of hard-wood, nailed a tin neck to it and attached some palm straw strings."

With that monster, he accompanied *Compay cotunto*, a native of Isle of Pines who became well known in Havana during the heyday of the *son*. Pelayo himself sang some of the montunos that reached the Isle from Havana. On Isle of Pines couples danced to those montunos forming chains and circles. One of the montunos went like this:

> *Caimán, caimán, caimán del guayabal,*
> *cogiendodo guayabas verdes,*
> *cogiendo guayabas verdes,*
> *te coge la madrugá.*

(Alligator, alligator, alligator / in the guava catch, / picking green guavas, / the morning will find you.)

"That *caimán*, which was so popular in the 20's, we used to play it on the seat of a rawhide chair that we heated with fire to make it sound like a tumbadora."

ALL OVER THE CARIBBEAN

After spending three days lost in the maze of the small islands of the Canarreos group, and sighting in the distance the shores of the is-land, German geographer Alexander von Humboldt wrote that "only one large island, about four times larger than Martinique, whose arid mountains are crowned by majestic conifers, stands out in the midst of the maze. It is Isle of Pines, which Columbus called *the Evangelist* and which other 16th century navigators called *Santa María*."[1]

Today's Isle of Youth, located to the southwest of Cuba in the Carib-bean, went by many names, but the most sensational was Treasure

[1] Alexander von Humboldt, *Ensayo político sobre la isla de Cuba* (Political Essay on the Isle of Cuba), Paris, Lacointe y Lasserre, 1840, p. 304.

Island. With the Spanish conquest and colonization it became a haven and source of supply for the pirate ships that sacked the undefended coastal towns and the gold-laden brigantines that took New World riches to Spain.

Reputed to be a paradise because of its ample beaches, attractive coves and wealth of fish, the wooded island experienced an influx of people from other Caribbean islands including Grand Cayman. Cayman people founded the village of Jacksonville to the south, and they brought with them a rich folklore represented by the round dance, which was very similar to the sucu-sucu. Thus, the convergence of the two Caribbean rhythms, a music whose English lyrics were accompanied by the accordion, harmonica, violin, base and machete, and another whose melodic scheme and instrumental scheme resembled that of the *son*, grew more marked in time. Another key factor in the convergence was the close ties between Cayman and Jamaican people and Cubans from Oriente province who also went to Isle of Pines to try to make a living from fishing or charcoal making.

NO LAIRS FOR SNAKES

People say that a traitor served as inspiration for this popular sucu-sucu, *Los majases no tienen cueva* (Snakes have no more lairs). The traitor, one Felipe Blanco, guided the Spaniards to his own house, where he'd taken in some mambises who staged an uprising on July 26, 1896. The Pimienta brothers and a poet name Iturriaga were murdered and buried on the spot. Blanco, who had given them shelter and food, only to turn them in, became the target of this famous sucu-sucu:

> *Los majases no tienen cueva,*
> *Felipe Blanco se las tapó,*
> *se las tapó, se las tapó,*
> *se las tapó que lo vide yo...*

(Snakes have no more lairs, / Felipe Blanco covered them up, / and I saw him do it.)

Now, Pelayo sings this parody accompanied by a tres that he learned to tune by ear when he was a boy and made charcoal in the mangrove forests on the shore.

THE *CLAVE* CHORUS

WHAT a lovely *clarina* voice, as the singer easily deals with the high notes, while the clave chorus awaits the sign from the *tonista* or leading voice to begin the chorus.

They are clad in sober dark suits. They cradle their claves as they await the order of the director. Then a sustained, rhythmic part is begun by the "viola," a small drum with a single skin and a ribboned handle played by expert hands.

Some of them are old, yet they achieve the counterpoint with the soloist and support her with their baritone's voices. The clarina (woman singer) continues to predominate as she weaves the melodic line of the song recently written by the group's improviser who writes on a blackboard, in large letters, the lyrics they are already singing, after the "censor" authorizes it.

Only the discrete movement of women's hips contrasts sharply with the solemnity of the 10 men and 5 women who comprise the clave chorus of Sancti Spíritus, a town located in the central part of the island, the only one of its kind in the country.

The 20's was the golden age of the clave chorus, which works with a melodic structure of Catalunian and African origin and traces its beginnings to 1909 as a rumba chorus.

In crowded tenements in Havana, Matanzas and Sancti Spíritus, the rumba chorus appeared on the scene in the 19th century. The groups rehearsed right before Christmas, in decorated spaces filled with benches and presided over by a large blackboard.

One very old clave chorus was called La Violencia. All its members were of Carabalí origin. They organized carnival *comparsas* accompanied by different types of drums, and they often took part in serenades.

Some clarinas had such mighty voices that their high tones won out over the drums and the noisy merrymaking.

Ignacio Piñeiro, creator of the National Septet that bears his name, and who introduced the *son* in Havana, was once a lyricist of a clave chorus, and a fine improviser he was. Nieves Fresneda, top dancer of today's National Folklore Company, was once a clarina of a clave chorus. Miguel Campanioni and Rafael *(Teofilito)* Gómez, traditional trovadores and authors of two very popular numbers, *Mujer perjura* (Perjured Woman) and *Pensamiento* (Thought), were directors of the Sancti Spíritus clave chorus.

The lyrical songs sung by free urban Black people also shared the characteristics of the most venerable clave choruses. Those songs lacked rhythmic intention and were decidedly not dance tunes. An example is:

> *Si el huracán furioso destruyera*
> *las flores de tu jardín,*
> *no importa... pues queda*
> *buena semilla.*

(Never mind if the furious hurricane destroys the flowers of your garden... good seed remains.)

The best-known groups in Havana and Matanzas continued into this century, including the Arpa de Oro, Moralidad y La Juventud. The lyrics of their numbers covered a broad range of topics of popular interest, and have come down to us, thanks to the efforts of informants and the Sancti Spíritus clave chorus, pride of a city where Cuban music is very deeply rooted.

THE DÉCIMA AS BARB

A line of horse-drawn buggies filled with pretty young women put an end to the doldrums of the July noon in Victoria de las Tunas, in eastern Cuba.

The imposing caravan conducted by coachmen with horsewhips and escorted by a large cavalry comprised of local farmers, drove three or four times around the city with seven thousand square kilometers and 300,000 inhabitants and then set out upon the six-kilometer drive that would take them along a narrow trail to the home of *El Cucalambé*, amidst ceiba and flamboyan trees, tiny benches and tall lanterns, hung with outsize banners bearing verses of the poet.

A few minutes later, at *Cucalambé* Park, with its hotel and restaurant, artificial lake, snack bar and amphitheater, the caravana stops beyond a rustic bridge over the Cornito, the almost legendary river on whose banks the poet lived. The girls, who for seven days are "Flowers of Virana," take their place on the fabulous ruins with tiles as a carpet and discarded iron grilles. It is time to open the traditional week in tribute to Juan Cristóbal Nápoles Fajardo, *el Cucalambé*, the most authentic writer of Cuban décimas of the middle of the 19th century, the poet whose work is today still repeated by country singer-poets. He was the most lucid improviser when it came to speaking of the tragedy of the Cuban Indians, the savagery of the conqueror and the impetus of the native-born criollos who were already stamping the Cuban seal in their poetry.

Cucalambé Week has been celebrated annually since 1966 with the aim of highlighting the work of Juan Cristóbal Nápoles Fajardo, born in Las Tunas on July 1, 1829.

The program includes film showings, a book fair and sporting events at different places in the locality. Cucalambé Park, with its two access roads, cafeterias, snack bars, pre-Colombian style bridges, an amphitheater for ten thousand people and the restored house where the poet lived for nearly 30 years stands at the center of the tribute.

FROM A CUBAN GUAJIRO

Poet and critic Cintio Vitier wrote in his book *Lo cubano en la poesía* (Cuban Elements in Poetry): "El Cucalambé set forth the auditive island landscape: vegetable sounds, birdsong, sounds made by water or wind.... Shores, mountains, swamps, plains, woods all emerge in escaping airborne or liquid sounds."[1]

El Cucalambé's work also sets forth the personality of the Cuban farmer, his fierce devotion to the land, his simple way of expressing in décimas all sorts of events, a natural, sincere chronicler who thoroughly assimilated popular Cuban language.

Criollismo or the cult of Cuban things began to emerge in Cuba as a poetic current in 1608 with the publication of Silvestre de Balboa's long poem *Espejo de paciencia* (Mirror of Patience). Years later that line was adopted to a greater or lesser degree by Rubalcaba, Pobeda, Domingo del Monte, Fornaris and Juan Cristóbal Nápoles Fajardo. In that period there began to take shape the impetus of the criollo for shaping a nationality, which would win a place for itself in the insurgent struggle unleashed in the second half of the 19th century with the 1868 Independence War.

In 1848, *El Cucalambé*—the name comes from the word cook, in English and *calambé* (lioncloth) in a pre-Colombian language, and is,

[1] Cintio Vitier, *Lo cubano en la poesía*, Instituto Cubano del Libro, Havana, 1970, p. 169.

in addition, an anagram of "Cuba clamé" (I clamored for Cuba)—joined the insurgent movement, the aborted conspiracy led by Joaquín de Agüero, and wrote décimas and proclamations calling for struggle. The pre-Colombian theme became for him a revolutionary body of symbols and images shaped by faultless metrics. He used criollismo and *siboneísmo* to give expression to the new conception of the mambí which 20 years later, would become uppermost in the course of armed struggle.

As a social poet of boundless audacity, he indulged in satire in proregime guise, while writing as well about the protest of the plundered Indian chieftain, as in "El cacique de Maniabón" or the woes of the guajiro, and his spontaneous ways, which *El Cucalambé* did not imitate. Rather, he created from within the guajiro.

SONGS OF THE PEOPLE

Décima singers, improvisers, musicians and singers from several countries in Latin America celebrated for four nights with the songs and dances of Peru's *socavón*, Panama's *mejorana*, Venezuela's *pasaje* and Puerto Rico's plena, with the Cuban *punto guajiro*, interpreted by over a score of poet-singers and 25 country music groups, both professional and amateur. At *Cucalambé* Park during an afternoon full of festivities the participants invited by Casa de las Américas drafted a declaration stating that just as Our America is one, just as our blood, our history, our culture and our struggle is one, so is our song one, our Song of the Earth, born as the expression of the people of Latin America and today the tool and the arm that reaffirm our identity against the permanent alienation with which imperialism and the oligarchies seek to negate the most genuine values of the people.

The loving renditions of the work of *El Cucalambé*, in the daily presence of over 25,000 spectators each day in the huge amphitheater, and the House of Recitals, the ruins of the poet's house, the excursions of families from Las Tunas to the corner of their beloved poet, showed once again that the décima repeated with innocent pleasure by oral and written tradition for over a century and a half. *El*

Cucalambé Week has been celebrated annually since 1966

Cucalambé's décima, continues to hold a permanent place in the cultural heritage of the Cuban people, an astonishing chronicle which then had quite a dosage of what today is the Cuban nationality.

CUBA Internacional. October 1974

TONADAS OF TRINIDAD

T HE *tonadas* of Trinidad, in central Cuba, are as old as the pottery, adobe houses, crafts and exquisite mansions that stand intact in the upper part of the city, one of the first that were founded by the Spanish conquerors in the 16th century.

The tonadas trace their origins to the San Juan religious festivals introduced by the Spaniards. Burning a Judas figure and bathing to keep from getting parasites were the first ways in which the day was celebrated by the local people, who dedicated to it lengthy songfests and massive picking of *yerba bendita* or blessed herb.

The tonada singers left from the sectors of Jibabuco and Pimpá. In Pimpá they gathered under a tamarind tree that still exists, and accompanied by three different kinds of drums (*quinto, requinto, bombó*), they headed for the center of the town, together with the people in general, who also danced and sang.

After that came the contests of soloists, until the winning district of the city was decided. People sang all night and at dawn, they went down to the river to wash their faces to get rid of the bad spirits picked up in the street.

After the end of the Ten Years War (1868-1878) Francisco Garzón, a fine tonada singer, gathered a group of friends, handed them *cuña* drums of the sort used by Congo people from Africa for combat, distributed a quinto, a bombo, a güiro and a *guataca*, a metal hoe head. They then paraded along the main street singing the tonada:

Today the *tonada* and the *fandango* are the same

> *Viva el Siboney,*
> *viva por quien morir,*
> *viva nuestra bandera otra vez*
> *por la cual yo muero.*

(Long live the Siboney, / long live what's worth dying for, / long live our flag again, / our flag, for which I die.)

From then on the patriotic theme recurs in tonadas, with words like this:

> *Ya Cuba es libre. ¿Quién dice que no?*
> *Ya Cuba es libre. ¿Quién dice que no?*
> *Y si a ti te pregunta un español,*
> *tú le contestas tengo bandera azul, blanca,*
> *triángulo punzó.*

(Cuba is now free who denies it? / And if a Spaniard asks you, / say you have a white and blue flag with a red triangle.)

Today the tonada and the *fandango* are the same. This musical form in which the Spanish melodic line blends with the rhythmic playing of the associations of black slaves, continues to be sung by the old people in town, although since 1962 they have been joined by youngsters who seek to keep the tradition from dying.

So, when people speak of Trinidad, of Benito Ortiz, its 80-year-old primitive painter, its Main Square, La Popa Church, Desengaño Street, the Santander family of potters, and its special way of weaving, mention must be made of the famous tonadas that outline close to four centuries of history of the municipality of Trinidad, in Sancti Spíritus province, bathed by the Caribbean and bordered by the peaks of the Escambray mountains.

CUBA Internacional. October 1981

FROM THE DEPTHS OF A GUITAR

LEO Brouwer is one of the world's greatest guitarists. The composer of technically "fantastic" works and an exceptional figure in Cuban music, he is also a simple man obsessed by time and the impassioned quest for new forms and sounds.

From boyhood, and throughout his high-pressure career, he has learned the techniques of the cello, clarinet, bass, percussion and piano. He has composed for orchestra, written music for films and revolutionized the language of the guitar to such an extent that he shook the "avant-garde music" that broke the cultural cliches that heretofore held sway in Cuba and the rest of Latin America.

For a man who is so accustomed to dealing with microphones and record devices, it should have been easy for him to talk about himself and his work. But the contact of his words with a cassette has an effect. His permanent mobility is heightened and makes him express two or three works at the same time. That is his way of tackling life. And as if trying to explain that vehemence, he says he has always been obsessed with time because he is unwilling to lose any of it.

"That comes from my paternal grandfather, a half-mad Dutchman who did research in biology and zoology, wrote piles of books and rare theses on medicine, both human and veterinary, and copied music. He opened one of the first radio stations in Cuba and drove around Havana in a car that was ultramodern for the time. I think that the old man, buried day and night in books and papers (I do the same quite often) was my model. He was the one who instilled in me the thirst for knowledge that I've had since I was a child."

A WORLD OF SOUND

Leo Brouwer's apartment is furnished with good taste and a highly personal style. Huge bookcases with glass doors display books and art objects. He owns a Picasso ceramic and several originals of the finest Cuban painters. "I love painting," he says, after running his eyes over a monochrome by Acosta León and a hazy sketch by Fidelio Ponce. "I studied painting for six years but I realized that I was no good at expressing painting, all I could do was feel it."

Before settling down to talk in the appealing sitting room, under a lovely art nouveau lamp, Leo shows off his work room, a small space located on a landing of the building. He writes his compositions there, and he writes them directly on lined paper. He makes neither drafts nor needs an instrument to structure his work.

"I think that the speciality of classical guitarist is complex and rich," he says after showing me one of his four concert guitars, and its sound is beautiful indeed.

"I have a simple piece of advice for anyone who wants to become a classical guitarist: listen to chamber and symphony music, to pianists, violinists, saxophonists. Leave out the guitar as an element of indispensable comparison. If you're going to play a piece by Bach, listen to it on a cello. And learn to play an instrument from each family."

Worldwide, five guitar scores are sold for every two piano scores and for every violin score. These figures provide eloquent evidence that Brouwer is right when he says it is the instrument of this century in both the popular and classical fields.

Absolutely all the musical groups of the western hemisphere use the guitar. While before, the classical guitar was the exclusive province of the trovador, it has now ceased to be a mystery. The Japanese alone sell about half a million guitars a year.

The emptiness left by the death of his mother motivated Leo as a child to cling to the study of the guitar.

For the solitary, sad boy, the instrument became something like a fetish which, in the hands of his father, an outstanding amateur guitarist who played the classics by ear, took on a beguiling life of its own. Then, at the age of fourteen, the discovery of guitar Maestro Isaac Nicola revealed to him the true essence of the guitar.

"One day I heard Maestro Nicola play the most important composers of the Spanish Renaissance," says Leo, 30 years later. "That revealed to me a world of sound that I'd never imagined. It was the simultaneous discovery of all the phenomena of music in a race against time.

"I remember that I had neither the time nor the money to learn, nor to pay Professor Nicola, and that at night I copied feverishly the scores that I was unable to buy. At the same time I listened to lots of music, Bartok, Stravinsky. When I heard them for the first time, I felt the sound as a stupendous thing. Even today I compose in the same way. Although my works seem highly structured, sound is what interests me."

According to many classical and popular guitarists, the guitar is an intimate thing that accompanies them all over and when they play it, they feel it near their hearts. Many say that it is hard to handle and that each guitar is unique. For Brouwer, who studied it earnestly while he struggled to make a living, the guitar continues to be the fetish that his father gave him when he was a child in an attempt to fill the vacuum left by his monther's death.

I PREFER TEACHING

Maestro Leo Brouwer, the director of Cuba's National Symphony Orchestra, was born in Havana in 1939. He studied with Isaac Nicola, initiator of the present Cuban School of the Guitar, and he completed his formation as a composer at the Juilliard School of Music in New York and at the University of Hartford, in Connecticut, also in the United States.

Leo Brouwer gave his first concert in 1955 and after that he began to build up a repertoire for the classical guitar.

"The archives were still in the cathedrals and the libraries, and researchers were few and far between.

"Today over 200 chamber works and lute transcriptions have appeared. As soon as I began to compose I saw the world in a new way. I saw everything in terms of form and content although I still didn't have a clue about dialectics. I still had no political formation. Paradoxically, I began to acquire one when I went to the United States in 1959 to study integral composition.

"I should say that I haven't composed very much for the guitar. Although it does have a strong appeal, it is very limited and is harder to master in creation than an orchestra. In addition a single instrument is a line, and expression is thus much more ardous than with the colors, depth and textures of many others."

He says that his chief vocation is teaching, although he doesn't have enough time to devote to it. Nonetheless, he has transmitted to students from over 40 countries the style of the Cuban School of Guitar, a movement that arose and grew in the field of classical guitar thanks to the Revolution and which marches alongside the manysided development of Cuban music in the new and traditional trova and in the popular guitar.

In 1969 he founded and directed the Sound Experimentation Group of the Cuban Institute for the Film Art and Industry (ICAIC). In a year and a half he taught the basic technique of disciplines that covered seven years of learning. From that group came the musicians who generated the Nueva Trova Movement that is so popular in Cuba and elsewhere.

"I've always taught by using methods adapted from painting, for instance, Paul Klee's classes in the Bauhaus. I make use of any form to reach musical forms: the form of a tree or a leaf, the forms of geometric symbols. All that is also musical form."

SUBJUGATION AND SYMBIOSIS

Leo owes his sharp musical ear, which today, hears music in everything, to the sound of a perennial piano played by his grandmother Ernestina Lecuona.

"And I say hear because music is form and humans communicate with forms of language such as musical, literary and painting codes. I communicate directly with the guitar and indirectly with composition. I have confronted two worlds of sound and I have switched the guitar way of composing to the orchestra and vice versa. That is the heady result of the treatment of forms, structures and technical models."

Just as Brouwer has been able to shift to the guitar the sounds of electronics without having to transform the instrument, he has used aleatory forms and achieved "non-guitar" effects as playing with the bow, tapping with the box of the instrument, using metal and crystal objects like some rock performers.

"There are two ways for the musician to face the public. One is by mastering an inaccessible repertoire, and the other, by offering a unique personality thanks to the multiplicity of the repertoire. For instance, some musicians play the world's most difficult piece and become known for that. There are even some musicians who choose pieces that no one else plays."

He went on to stress that as a guitarist, he plays universal music, although his programs are characterized by some fairly uncommon specializations in antique and preclassical music. The important thing is to provide information to the audience.

"I've now spent ten years without interruption as a concert musician, and I feel hypertrophied. That's why I cancelled everything for a year. Meanwhile, I'm composing a lot and preparing a new repertoire."

A CUBAN GUITARIST

As a Paris critic noted several years ago: "Leo Brouwer took the guitar out of the Andalusian ghetto and made it universal and contemporary." A letter from Emilio Pujols, student of Francisco Tárrega, the creator of the modern guitar school, contains this praise to Leo Brouwer: "Since Debussy's *Homage to Manuel de Falla*, there hadn't been a work for guitar like Leo Brouwer's *Canticum*, which has also become another point of departure."

Leo Brouwer is one of the world's greatest guitarists

In addition critics in France, England, the United States and Canada have said that Brouwer's works have also been a point of departure for the contemporary universal repertoire as well.

All that is pleasing to this modest man, who demands that all the promotional material on his appearances in other countries states that he is a *Cuban* guitarist.

"Fame hasn't made me conceited. As they say, fame is ephemeral, it's a great moment that could lead to the perdition of a person who rests on his laurels."

Leo finds it hard to pinpoint the high points of his musical career, but says that the first was his first tour, back in 1970. He attended the world premiere of one of his compositions in Berlin's Comic Opera. He also met Paul Dessau, one of the greatest composers of the century, and early one morning, he heard a nightingale sing.

"It was an extremely heady contact with success. Four months of hard work in God knows how many cities and countries. Another

135

important moment in my career was when I gave in London a complete concert, a cycle of great composers of the 20th century, including Stockhausen, Boulez, Bussotti, Takemitsun and Barraqué.

"I'm not about to rate them, history will take care of that. Let me say, however, that Stockhausen and Boulez are regarded as the two key composers of the second half of this century.

"And the fact that some people have placed me in their category is a great source of pride...."

CUBA Internacional. November 1982

OF MEN AND GODS

IT was the first sunny day of Spring 1964 in Paris when the recently-created National Folklore Company of Cuba arrived at Orly airport.

Those men and women of the people, who had worked at the most modest jobs, could hardly fail to be amazed at the revelation of the City of Lights in spring.

Not many hours before, they had left the strong sun of their country and received a taste of the crude Canadian winter during a stopover. And now they found themselves in the tenuous sunlight in which the Parisians basked in the parks and boulevards. In a word, the Cubans had in a brief period of time come into contact with the rigors and the sweetness of the seasons, something that is beyond the reach of stay-at-homes in the Caribbean.

That first tour was perhaps the most exciting of all for those performers who had launched, spontaneously and with great love of tradition, the long series of successes of the Company, which has already celebrated its 20th anniversary.

The Company's senior members remember that first international tour, which was followed by 25 more. They all agree that their success overwhelmed them as they performed their Cuban songs and dances of African and Hispanic roots, of both a secular and religious nature. Never before had the cultural tradition of Cuba, its customs and street vendors'songs, its rhythmic and melodic language, been presented with such authenticity before a European audience.

In 1964 their appearances in the International Festival of the Sara Bernhardt National Theater, to which they had been invited, proved insufficient. With the same excitement and expressive force with which they danced on the stage they performed in communist municipalities, in public squares and also on French television.

They all remember a chilly, grey day when they danced in an open plaza surrounded by a large number of passersby. Despite the weather the half-naked, barefoot dancers performed the Yoruba beat dictated by drums played by expert hands. The powerful rhythm and the enviable voice of the soloist who told legendary tales of Africa, the bodies of the dancers who quickly warmed up with their difficult choreography, all received thunderous applause. The show was so impressive that one of the numerous flower vendors of the city commented: "These people could wake up a cemetery."

She neatly summed up the impression made on the public by the Company, which since then (April 1964) has performed in over 200 cities around the world.

THE VOICE OF YEMAYÁ

Lázaro Ross waxes nostalgic over his youth, when he was regarded as a virtuoso dancer specializing in Oggún and Obbatalá, Yoruba deities.

However, Lázaro, a founding member of the Company and one of the few informants who contributed to the ongoing research required for its development, still has a voice with a broad range and a metallic timbre in which strength is linked with a great sense of rhythm. In other words, the voice that Cuban musical folklore requires.

"At first, we sang without microphones, so you can imagine how the voice needed to stand out above the drums. Because I was a dancer in the early days, I do a better job in stage expression now. I was the one who sang for Nieves Fresneda, that great dancer of ours, who can't be equalled in dancing Yemayá in the *Yoruba Suite*."

Lázaro is the only remaining informant of the original founders of the Company. His outstanding memory is of that first tour, when he, who supported his family with his cook's salary, suddenly found himself overnight before the Cuban public and then, a year later, in France, Algeria, Belgium and Spain, on the Company's first international tour.

"The collective interest that bound us then, and which continues to prevail today, was and is unquestionably the key to our success. A dancer is sometimes a soloist and sometimes a member of the chorus, without any notions about stardom, in the conviction that all roles are important and that what counts is what the audience receives.

"Some Africans who saw us in Paris were surprised when they found they could understand the songs sung in their own dialects, and they asked us how our people had managed to maintain that tradition with a fidelity that somewhat took them aback, but which made us feel very proud."

Lázaro Ross has also worked as a choreographer, to the great benefit of the Company, thanks to his knowledge as a dancer. This tireless worker, who last year received the National Culture Order, conferred by the Cuban government upon outstanding artists, artistic groups and intellectuals, says it was the best reward imaginable for his years of hard work.

"That was the happiest moment of my life," he says modestly. "And not only for me, but for my mother as well. Seeing me decorated publicly by the Revolution, because my work is looked upon as a contribution to the art and culture of my people, was more than what she could ever have dreamed of wanting."

THE GENUINELY CUBAN

Until the creation of the National Folklore Company in 1962 in Cuba there was no artistic institution devoted to the collection and revival of the people's musical and dance heritage.

Before Fernando Ortiz, a brilliant scholar who salvaged dances and songs of African origin and organized lectures illustrated by live,

OLGA FERNÁNDEZ

authentic performers, no one had gone beyond the external, picturesque side of popular creation.

The tendency to falsify the truly Cuban nature of traditional culture
disappeared with the victory of the Revolution. Three years after that
far-reaching event, in 1962, at the initiative of two young men, Mexican choreographer Rodolfo Reyes and Cuban folklorist Rogelio
Martínez Furé, the National Folklore Company was created. The press
carried a call to which nearly 500 hopefuls responded. The more
than thirty members of the dance troupe were chosen from among
workers, students, domestic servants, laundresses and a few members of amateur groups who made sporadic appearances sponsored
by the Department of Folklore of the National Theater.

"At first it was hard to find people who knew folkloric dances and
songs," says Martínez Furé, now the folklore consultant to the Company and to Contemporary Dance of Cuba, a separate company.

"We tested them for their sense of rhythm and knowledge of basic
steps in dance folklore to come up with a selection of the best dancers, singers and percussionists. Two or three of the percussionists
mastered the art of making drums, some of which are highly complex, such as the *batá* and *arará* drums[1], while others served as informants on everything pertaining to the manifestations of African culture in our country."

Once the group was created, its members began a rigorous training
that included classes on history of the dance, Marxism and folklore, in
addition to daily practice. People who knew one or another song or
dance through practice in the family or imitation thus acquired a fuller
information. In time true artists were created who had a professional,
modern sense of theater.

"We didn't settle for people knowing how to dance in the Yoruba
tradition, or the rumba and guaguancó," added Martínez Furé. "We
wanted them to know how and why these dances existed in Cuba, the
meaning of the steps and movements, the text of the songs. Later we
completed that instruction with the compiling of data supplied by our
informants on the dress, colors, hair styles and symbolism of all the
elements in the staging. After that, we were ready to stage our first

[1]See "The Batá Drums" in this book. "—Ed."

140

production. It was comprised of three separate but complementary cycles: 'Yoruba', 'Congo'and 'Rumbas and Comparsas,' which became a classic in the Company's repertoire since its first showing on July 25, 1963, in Havana's Mella Theater. We've been staging it for over two decades."

Fernando Ortiz used to say that Cuban musical folklore is social in character, that group singing and dancing are more common than individual ones. This principle is followed by the Company, which has staged Cuban country numbers such as the zapateo, punto guajiro, dances and instrumentals of the Tumba Francesa and the Carabalí Izuamá Group, which still prevail in Santiago, in Eastern Cuba. Although only a handful of researchers are working on folklore with informants, the quest for venerable tradition continues.

TRINITARIAS

After its first showings Trinitarias was rated a definitive work by the critics. Sharing the program with it was another number by Choreographer Ramiro Guerra, Sayings, Old Saws and Tongue-twisters, based on material collected by late research-writer Samuel Feijóo. It includes gems of popular humor that illustrate an old Cuban saying: sayings have to hit the nail on the head.

Trinitarias made a fine closing for the celebration of the Folklore Company's 20th anniversary. It is a vast fresco of Cuban popular culture with manifestations of traditions and folklore of Central Cuba, especially the old colonial city of Trinidad.

The first part of Trinitarias included street vendors'calls, an exact rendition of the local Royal Congo grouping, the country tunes of the area and Taita (literally Papa) Lanza's parranda or country festival. The second part included Trinidad Trova, the comparsas of Los Pitos and El Cocuyé, ending with the local religious festivity, the San Juan.

The image of the old city, one of the first towns founded by the Spaniards, which was based on the work of primitive painter Benito Ortiz, a native of Trinidad, provided the backdrop for the final production staged by the National Folklore Company.

THE DIFFICULT ART OF THE DRUM

"Playing batá drums in Africa after all those centuries since they were taken to America, astonished the Algerians," says Carlos Aldama, leading percussionist of the National Folklore Company.

He is a profound connoisseur of those drums of Yoruba origin, used traditionally in Cuba to accompany the songs and dances of the syncretic religion known as *santería*.

"I was born in a poor district of Havana, where I learned to play the quinto and conga drums, dance the rumba, the guaguancó and some Afro rhythms. I loved the batá drums best because of their melodiousness and their complexity. To master more than 300 pieces played by this family of drums, first you have to learn to play the *okónkolo*, the smallest of the three, then move on to the *itótele* and finally, the *iyá*. The learning process takes about six years."

Carlos Aldama belonged to one of the groups that performed in the National Theater, headquarters of the Folklore Department headed by ethnologist and musicologist Argeliers León.

"Before, playing the batá had a religious connotation. They could be built only by specialists, like the late Trinidad Torregrosa. Now, all the percussionists of our Company, and even some of our dancers and singers, know how to make a drum. We know the pieces played on a wide range of drums, some of them peculiar to a given geographic area of Cuba. We also use instruments that you no longer find in their original setting, such as the marímbula, a wooden box with metal strips that acted as bass in country music and the son montuno."

The outstanding percussionist says that the Company has been like a school for him, just as it is for young graduates of the National School of Art who join it. A tailor's assistant in his youth, Carlos Aldama never dreamed he'd lay down his needle and thread to catch a plane to some of Europe's great cities, with their great theaters. Much less did he ever dream he'd study music in a conservatory.

"I never imagined my whole life would change when I was 24 years old. And I don't mean only in connection with my work as a musician, but also my complete involvement in the revolutionary process."

A CARIBBEAN PANTHEON

The National Folklore Company completed the celebration of its 20th anniversary with a massive comparsa that burst right through the doors of the Mella Theater, in a rhythmic tumult staged by the members of the Company and the audience of *Trinitarias*.

The audiences that filled the theater night after night saw a fine program: the return of the "Yoruba," "Congo" and "Rumbas and Comparsas" cycles and the first performance of *Sayings, Old Saws and Tongue-twisters* and *Trinitarias*, both with choreography by Ramiro Guerra.

"Yoruba," "Congo" and "Rumbas and Comparsas": good test for artistical precision, which characterizes this Company since its foundation, though on this occasion the artists were mainly composed of graduates of the National School of Art, whose technique is more pure than that of their predecessors, spontaneous artists who gave what is genuinely folkloric.

In the "Yoruba" cycle, Elegguá, the first and last of the deities of Cuba's santería pantheon, opens the ceremonial festival. He opens the roads with his forked stick so that the other *orishas* or saints can come in. Another dancer is Obbatalá, the wisest of all, the creator of humans, an ancient, eternal orisha sung to by a chorus of seven women clad in white, the orisha's color.

Now the waves of the sea emerge in the shape of billowing blue cloth. Yemayá, the top female deity of the Yoruba pantheon, appears, interpreted by Margarita Ugarte, worthy successor to the unforgettable Nieves Fresneda.

Yemayá is followed by Changó, god of fire and virility, accompanied by ten male dancers who burst on the scene like incandescent darts. His dance is violent and aggressive, while the axe, a phallic symbol, traces arabesques in the air.

The aim in presenting once again those three independent though complementary cycles, according to their author, Rogelio Martínez Furé, is to offer a wide panorama of Cuban religious and profane dance creations.

The first part symbolizes the world of the gods, the mythical, the unreal. The second represents humans in contact with the earth, and

National Folklore Company of Cuba, institution devoted to the collection and revival of the Cuban people's musical and dance heritage

the dances of the slave-owners and the slaves. The third signifies the joy of the human being in breaking with religious and social bonds through the drums and the conga, elements of the most popular festivity.

Along with other popular creations, this rich, varied cycle has withstood the test of time.

SETTING: OLD HAVANA

Drumbeats sound in the Plaza de Armas (Arms Square), in the lovely inner courtyard of the old Place of the Captains General just as they used to sound on the Epiphany, on January 6, the only occasion that slaves were allowed to have fun and play their music openly.

All possible Cuban instruments join their voices in this concert of percussion folklore presented by the Company in Old Havana.

The dancers show the magical danzón and the hot rumba, and they throw themselves into the rhythm with all the expressiveness of their faces and bodies while the stupendous voice of soloist Lázaro Ross and the hands of the magnificent percussionists achieve an air of enchantment.

In any manifestation of purely Cuban music, the performance of the Company is absolutely brilliant. They close the performance with the traditional, legendary comparsa El Alacrán, staged along a stretch of Obispo Street that has been restored to its 19th century look.

The throng of people who flood the plaza and the street to see the National Folklore Company love and respect its members, who mean so much to the perpetuation of the values of the people, the only creator of popular art. The National Folklore Company. which has been awarded the National Culture Order, faithfully transmits and spreads the dances, customs, music and songs that for centuries pointed the way of truly Cuban culture.

CUBA Internacional. October 1982

WHEN YEMAYÁ DANCES

INCREDIBLY the tiny, light-stepping 80-year-old lady, with shining little eyes, was the top woman dancer of the National Folklore Company. She was also the best oral historian on the rituals and customs of the men and women brought from Africa in the holds of the slave ships. She was the best exponent of *Lucumí* or Yoruba dancers of the oldest type of danzón, but most of all, she is the supreme embodiment of the all-wise Yemayá.

When Nieves Fresneda danced Yemayá, goddess of the sea and fecundity in Yoruba mythology, her blue gown dipped and swollen in imitation of the sea. When this agile woman's body bended as if she were emerging from the ocean bottom, the rhythmic expressiveness of Afro dancing was highlighted once again.

That day Nieves Fresneda was not wearing her blue gown with silvery strips that imitates imaginary waves. Her jet black hair was not covered with her blue headscarf. She was then a youthful old woman who seasoned her story with appealing anecdotes. She was formally retired, but she still worked with the National Folklore Company, which she helped to bring into being at the start of her successful career at the surprising age of 62.

OUR IDEA OF FUN BACK THEN

"Whenever researchers would come around the neighborhood to get information, people always said, 'Go see Nieves, she used to live with black people born in Africa.' That's how they found me, not long after the Revolution, when researchers wanted to learn about African traditions, rites and customs.

"That was how I started to work with Argeliers León, then director of the National Theater's Department of Folklore. I used to demonstrate the Lucumí dances in a lecture series on songs and legends of Cuba. In the theater's smaller hall, the Covarrubias, I performed for the first time on a stage the Afro dances that have contributed as much to our music.

"Then, in 1962, the National Folklore Company was founded. I was a solo dancer with them until two years ago. Sure, I know they say that old people need to stay active to keep from dying in some corner, but the fact of the matter is that these legs of mine just aren't fit for fancy footwork any more."

Her memory, however, was fit indeed. Her earliest memories of the crowded tenement where she was raised were very precise and detailed, as she described those February evenings at the beginning of carnival, evenings inhabited by Lucumí women whose faces had been scarred at birth, freedwomen who wore full, starched white gowns, cheap metal hoop earrings, coral beads and very fine embroidered headscarves.

"Those Lucumí women," Nieves recalled, "would be out on the street since the night before with their little tables and charcoal burners to sell their wares, including fritters made of black-eyed peas, that was their specialty.

"They were very dignified those Lucumí black women. And then there was an impressively tall man known as the Elephant who played the cymbals with great verve while his wife performed elegantly on the hand organ, with the fritter women calling out their delicacies in the background.

"So, when I was a girl of 9 or 10, I learned the vendors' calls, which I'd hum later on in the courtyard of our tenement. I also learned the steps of the rumba which I saw people dance every Sunday, when I escaped the watchful eye of my grandfather, a freedman who still wore a hoop in one ear, the mark of his former master. I loved to go to the *bembé*, fiestas dedicated to the orishas, the gods of each ethnic grouping of blacks.

"That was what we did for fun back then, and we young people from the tenement house sure had a lot of fun with all the festivities that went on. It never entered my mind that all the things I was learning would one day help us to salvage and revive our Afro-Cuban traditions."

RETIREMENT... ON PAPER

Nieves was amazing as she told about the festivities in her district, the centrally located, populous Pueblo Nuevo sector of Havana, the characteristics of her tenement, aptly named Africa: it was divided by two inner courtyards that set off the territories of the Congos, the Lucumís and the Chinese, who wore their hair in cues and carried their wares in large baskets.

"Every May 20, the blacks in my tenement brought out some huge drums called tahonas and to the accompaniment of cowbells, they played a conga that all the local people joined immediately. We headed for another barrio whose entrance was decorated with flower arches. Under them we'd improvise complicated rumbas or the most difficult guaguancó. The best poets and dancers were the ones who won victory for the district.

"Like my Mama, I was a clarina, the leading voice of the clave chorus. The chorus, which was very popular at the time and went back to the 19th century, also sang to Cuba, national heroes and the Yara Revolution[1]. Every December 23, we went out to sing. We'd sing at name day festivities, finishing on December 25. The director was always given a rosette made of woven ribbons that contained Spanish gold

[1]Cuba's 1868 Independence War against Spain. "—T."

coins. I was the leading dancer of the comparsa of Las Guaracheras (literally, women who sing and dance the guaracha) and I won several prizes for rumba dancing. In 1937 I organized Las Bolleras comparsa, an exact copy of the customs of the Lucumí black woman with whom I was raised. Like them, I hawked the fritters and then sold them and did my dance in my dress decorated with ribbons.

"The carnivals from 37 to 40 were the best of the time. They were held all along the Prado and the Malecón sea drive. The streamers used to get so snarled that you'd have to cut through them with your body to be able to move. Back then, a street comparsa called Los Kokoricamos, men who wore tunics made of strips of cloth and a hood over their heads that twisted their faces out of shape, often caused a panic among the spectators. That comparsa's only music was beating on frying pans.

"I used to climb up on the piece of the old city wall that still stands opposite the former Presidential Palace, now Museum of the Revolution, to call out my vendor's cry. Now, no exaggeration, my fine voice could be heard over all that noise. And finally, I'd sell all my fritters to the public who gathered around to listen to me."

Nieves Fresneda delved into another memory, the way the Company's performance and her own dancing were hailed in over 15 countries of Europe and Africa and the ovation she received for her Yemayá in the Theater of the Nations in Paris, the first stop on the tour. She remembered the demonstrations of affection of the former Soviet audiences and a tribute she received in 1964 when she danced in Algeria.

But of all of the tributes, she had a special place in her memories for the tribute that the Ministry of Culture held for her in 1978, when she retired from the stage. That night she danced for the last time, in the presence of her colleagues and students, the dances that brought her fame. But more than a farewell performance—she is still on the Company roster, at her own insistence—the event was a recognition that brought her higher praise than any other.

THAT'S WHAT LIVING IS ALL ABOUT

"Now I only dance in performances where I don't have to move too much, for instance, I'm the Carabalí Queen in a ballet the Company is currently staging. I'm solemn as a queen, but an Africa queen, after all, so I do a few steps to the beat of a drum.

"I think that a person needs to feel the music to be a good dancer. If they don't, they can't dance, become transfigured, actually turn into the character.

"I've danced Ochún, goddess of love, Elegguá, he who clears the roads. Each one has his or her steps and music. But I like Yemayá, the Great Mother, the Mistress of the Sea, above all.

"When I was a young girl, I danced lots of danzón and contradanza, the *yambó*, a dance from the days of Spanish rule, very elegant. We girls wore Catalonian lace gowns and the men wore tails."

This woman who was born with the century, who lived in Havana right after the end of colonial rule, who had the privilege of witnessing the most popular manifestations of Cuban colonial culture, also had a treasure trove of stories about the fighting attitudes of the Cubans at the turn of the century as the people expressed their opposition to the United States intervention and the corrupt government that sold out the fledgling Republic.

Nieves, who worked for years in the home of poet and political leader Rubén Martínez Villena, knew a great deal about the courage and dignity of revolutionaries. At the militant burial of the ashes of communist leader Julio Antonio Mella, she saw that many people opposed the status quo. She experienced extreme poverty when she worked as an ironer in a laundry in order to support, first, her sisters and brothers, and then, her children.

She said happily: "I have the honor of having helped the National Folklore Company become what it is today, a group of recognized international fame. And I'm proud of having worked with researchers such as Cuba's great scholar, Don Fernando Ortiz, and many other specialists who have enriched the studies on our folklore.

"At least I know, and this is what matters, that I haven't lived in vain. I know that something of me will remain in dance and in books."

Nieves Fresneda, the best exponent of Lucumí or Yoruba dances

NIEVES FRESNEDA: A LIVING LIBRARY

Folklorist Rogelio Martínez Furé regarded Nieves Fresneda as the "leading woman dancer in Cuban folklore and the one who has contributed the most to our knowledge of dances of Yoruba and Arará background, as well as of the danzón.

"For 20 years Nieves not only provided solid information to musicologists and folklorists, she not only danced like a virtuoso, but she also taught in the National School of Art, the Company's own school, in Modern Dance and the National Ballet. She has also participated in courses to train art instructors for the amateur movement, and she has always been very willing to contribute her knowledge on dress, hairstyles, a type of meal, any sort of oral tradition."

Martínez Furé added: "I don't think she had any equal in her Yemayá, in the *Yoruba Suite*, not only because of the way in which she performed traditional steps but because of the creativity and talent she contributed at every turn.

"Nieves danced better than anyone that had become milestones in the history of Cuban folklore. She deserves recognition for having offered her invaluable knowledge to the development of this cultural manifestation of our people.

"I called her a living library, one of the learned old people of traditional Cuban culture."

CUBA Internacional. June 1981

THE BATÁ DRUMS

"**M**Y father was born a slave. He told me that my grand-father, a Lucumí prince, was grabbed on a river bank while he was bathing with Ochún, a goddess of ours who wandered around the savannah and the forest and then blended into the waters of the river in her yellow-green tunic.

"Grandfather swore to Papa that when that pretty, laughing woman danced, the sun came out and the rain multiplied the trees and the lakes. She seemed to move through the air with her head full of garlands made of stars and moonlight. None of the men of his retinue or the whites who captured him saw Ochún that afternoon. She was invisible to all other mortals. And grandfather cried when they sepa-rated him from her and carried him off in an overcrowded ship. I think that the unbounded sadness of the prince, who watched with tear-filled eyes the coast of his realm disappear in the distance, made him cling to the small drum that one of his warriors carried. He heard it above the moans of the dying people who were cast into the sea, and he felt less alone during the crossing.

"Once in Cuba, before the warrior was taken to a sugarmill by a white man who chose him for his strength from among hundreds of slaves, he gave the drum to his prince. Grandfather learned to make them and he taught his family. He spent night after night with his drums. He hollowed them out with rudimentary tools, and because they were made of mahogany, a hardwood, they survived.

"Papa says that years and years of tanning goatskins, narrowing the waist of the drums, similar to a woman's waist, and beating the hides of his sacred batá drums, finally deformed grandpa's hands and that the day he went with him to the river and showed him the forest path that led to the mambises and freedom, grandfather suddenly grew old. He grew old, but he carried on making drums that were the messengers of the Yoruba gods, with the secret aim of once again calling up Ochún and running with her, holding hands, through the woods that loomed beyond the slave barrack."

TO FORGET THE WHIP

Tens of thousands of people who were hunted down like animals and bought as cheap goods were brought to Cuba from different points of Africa's west coast. The shiploads of Congo, Carabalí, Arará, Mandinga and Lucumí people included their languages, religions, dances, music and instruments.

The first manifestation of African art in the Antilles was the building of those instruments and then, religious fetishes and attributes. The three pillars of their cultural identity, music, song and religion, sound, rhythm and superstition, would be handed down through the centuries.

Thanks to the presence of their cultural characteristics, it was possible to determine the geographic and ethnographic identity of the groups of people who arrived from Africa. Each shipload must have included either musical instruments typical of each group of people or the persons who knew how to build them. Evidence of this is to be found in accounts quoted by Alexander von Humboldt and then by Fernando Ortiz of the ways the slavers forced their captives with whips to dance on the crowded deck of the ships.

Later on the slave owners learned that song and dance provided noisy consolation to their chattels.

Under the inhuman system of forced labor, some slaves committed suicide, and even the strongest grew less productive. So, as a way of easing the prisonlike existence of the slave quarters and encouraging the efforts of the people who cut the sugarcane and turned the grinding machinery, they were allowed to play their drums and organize in cabildos according to their ethnic origin. Although in July 1839 the Captain General of the Island authorized Africans to hold celebrations in keeping with the customs of their country, the practice was already frequent in the slave quarters. And the drum, the most primitive of their musical instruments, the symbol of royal or military authority, the main instrument in African music, which was regarded as more noisy than beautiful because it seemed to make noise instead of producing pleasant sounds, became the collective sounding box of human groups who refused to disappear.

HONOR TO THE ORISHAS

"Grandfather lighted the dark slave barrack with large gourds filled with fireflies and candles that the master gave him for the saints in his own private chapel. There was a reason for that:

"Because they couldn't play their drums or sing to their orishas—the master said it was a way of sending messages from one plantation to another to stage uprisings and organize communities of runaway slaves, the *palenques*—they took cover behind the Catholic saints and found resemblances between Changó and Santa Bárbara, Ochún and the Virgin of Charity and Obbatalá and the Virgin of Mercy. That enabled them to survive and even forget for a few hours the scars left by the stocks or the whip. That was how grandfather was able to continue to build his sacred drums dedicated to the orishas, who are like we ourselves. Some of them laugh heartily like Ochún, others are delicate like Elegguá, lord of the roads, or they sit in a palmtree when they're angry, like Changó, lord of lightning. They act like people, they eat and make love, they're jokers and they're cruel, they're weak and they're warlike. Grandfather was the one who knew them well, he was the only one who could reach them and bring them down from the *ilé* with his drum playing."

A CONCERT FOR SIX HANDS

The Lucumí arrived in Cuba probably in the 16th century, although the batá drums, according to Fernando Ortiz, "did not arrive with their form and sacred character until the 19th century. Ortiz explains that the reason was probably that some drummers of añá (those with the proper personal and religious characteristics) were brought to Cuba as slaves, after the destruction of the capital of the Lucumís by the Fulas (Peules) in 1825... That event explains the great abundance of Lucumís who were brought to Havana and Matanzas by the slave trade."[1]

What is undeniable is that the Lucumís, people with greater cultural development than other African nations, had the richest religious cults in terms of liturgy, instruments, music, song and dance. Subsequently, after a process of transculturation and syncretism, the Yoruba or Lucumí religion, based on devotion to orishas or saints, came to be identified with elements of Catholicism, to become the Cuban religion known as *Regla de Ocha* or Santería.

In Cuba the batá drums are used in the orisha cults. They are three in number, with skins at both ends, and they are played horizontally on the drummers' legs, or hanging from their neck by straps. The use of two skins of different diameters, and the variable height at which the drum is played, enriches its tonalities. The batá drums are regarded as the most melodic of drums, and they are complex, with their hundreds of pieces, in a true "concert for six hands" because of the registers they attain.

The iyá, Yoruba word for mother, is the largest and principal drum with its acute and grave voice. The itótele, the medium-size drum, is grave on sound and takes the part of the bass, while the *okónkolo*, also known as *omelé*, is the smallest, makes the highest note, equivalent to a bugle because of the acuteness of its timber.

The skin of the batá drums is tensed or tuned using strips of bull skin, and their shape resembles that of an hourglass. The big iyá has bells

[1]Fernando Ortiz, *Los instrumentos de la música cubana* (Instruments of the Cuban Music), Havana, Ed. Cárdenas y Cía., Vol. IV, 1954, p. 315.

(*chaguoró*) on the edge to add new sounds to the group of drums. The largest skin of the iyá is rubbed with a resin prepared with a ritual formula to cushion its vibration. This process gives the big drum sounds with a dry timber.

According to Yoruba tradition, an orisha lives in the batás, especially in the iyá. That is their secret, or *añá*. And the ritual of batá building calls for animal sacrifices to feed the drum just as is done with the gods. In addition the drummers must refrain from sexual intercourse and consult the sacred skins that speak the Lucumí language.

While traditionally the building and playing of the drums were limited to the *olú-batá*, or initiates, today this is not the case. Fernando Ortiz provided an account of the first time that he placed the batá drums and their music before a secular audience.

After that, 1936, the batás would illustrate his lectures on the Yoruba universe, although they had to "convince" the black gods through prayers and sacrifices, because they took a dim view of the attempt at simony. Ortiz said they favored them with their authorization to hear the sacred drums and sacred songs containing beautiful portions of the vast lucumí hymnal, as long as it was for cultural purposes.

Traditionally, the drummers learned their art by ear, while today, many of the percussionists of the National Folklore Company have added to their traditional knowledge the study of music. That is the best way to perpetuate the different rhythmic styles of Carabalí, Congo and Lucumí origin, because each culture brought from Africa its instruments, songs, dances, timbers and melodic structures that now form part of Cuba's folkloric heritage.

ON THE ROAD WITH OCHÚN

"Papa used to say that before he learned to speak like a Christian, he helped my grandfather line the drums, put on their skins and tune them with strips of hide. It seems that Changó, the god of music, gave my grandfather a special gift for building batá drums. For him everything had a voice: the hoot of an owl, the rumble of thunder, the

157

cry or whistle of birds, the fury of a hurricane. Grandfather even imitated the roar of the lion of the jungles of his native land with his magic drums. Now, he never sang or danced, he just played his drums as if he were asleep. Then only his hands were alive as they leaped over the skins like a restless animal. Grandfather's batás spoke Lucumí, they conversed among themselves and brought down the gods who took possession of the bodies of humans. That is what Papa saw when he was a boy. He saw how grandfather cared for the batás as if they were orishas, once they were initiated. He'd bring them down from the ceiling to eat the goat that he slaughtered for them. He kept them hung from the ceiling, like the clouds that bring Changó's thunder. They could not be allowed to touch the floor, so the drummers tied them to their bodies. That way they could play the batá on their knees, without worrying about dropping it.

"When Papa came back from the 1898 Independence War, the slaves were free and in the barracks he found only the very oldest people. Grandfather had chosen the solitude of a tiny plot of land, far from the mill. He took with him the secret of his drums, his patience in making them. One day he promised Papa that he'd teach him to play the okónkolo.

"Papa had to learn to sit properly, place his hands correctly and hum the songs to make sure he did not get lost in the music. After a year of daily practice Papa knew how to play the okónkolo and he played as a duo with grandfather's itótele. And, although the okónkolo is almost always the batá that starts playing, in a piece called *cheche bururú* to greet Ochún, it was grandfather's itótele that began.

"Papa came to be a master, an olu-batá of a Lucumí cabildo (lodge). His set of batás did not need to go through a special initiation at the cabildo, because they were grandfather's and more than sanctified. They were original batás. Grandfather was happy because he knew that the roads of his orishas would not be lost.

"The day that Papa sat opposite him and played his drum until midnight like a past master, grandfather put Ochún in all the *canistel* trees of the yard, sat down on a chair and let himself be carried away by Ochún."

BATÁ STYLE

The sound of the batá drums may be compared with that of an orchestra. They comprise an orchestra of three drums with bells added, known as the *chaguoró*. In this orchestra, the iyá occupies the center, with the itótele to its left and the okónkolo to its right. The measures of each drum are inalterable when they are used in rituals, and any alteration makes them profane, non-sacred. Formerly, they used to belong to the Yoruba cabildo but subsequently, they could be taken from one place to another. Because of the high cost of the drums and the specialization required of the drummers, batá players were hired for different festivities, and the remuneration of these priests was modest: 21 pesos and 21 five-cent pieces at each ceremony, plus the abundant food offered to the orishas and their devotees in the home of the *santero* or official of the Yoruba cult.

Fernando Ortiz pointed out in his essay on the batá drums that by 1953 the Afro-Cuban batás had left Havana to take part in a show in the United States, where they played with great success in Las Vegas. The batás undoubtedly faced the almost insurmountable difficulty, which at bottom was economic in nature, of the shortage of olú-batá drummers and the virtual impossibility that any of them join a great symphony orchestra. He went on to recall what happened to musician Gilberto Valdés, when he tried to bring to the orchestra Afro-Cuban percussion in the batá style: the inability of the drummers to read music limited the original idea.

Outside of Havana and Matanzas, in western Cuba, this type of drum does not exist in America. However, in Brazil, where the Yoruba influence was profound, there are similar drums. But even in those areas of marked Lucumí presence at the time of the slave trade, other batás were used, in an effort to replace the authentic ones, but they failed to imitate the sound of the waters where Ochún bathes or the thunder sent by Changó from on high, thunder that moves through the forest and reaches the hermetic drums, which open their hearts only to the orishas.

The batá drums

OMELÉ

"I guess I have in my blood that gift of grandfather's and Papa's, because I'm really good at drums. I was raised with drums, hearing them and playing them by ear. I've known the greats: Papa Silvestre, Trinidad Torregrosa, *El Sublime* Andrés, *El Sordo* Juan. Others died of old age playing the okónkolo. They could not make it to the *itótele*, much less the iyá. As an itótele player, I have to keep on my toes, because the iyá is always calling to the itótele, who has to respond in the changes of rhythm.

"I learned when I was a little boy that drums are men's business. My sisters weren't allowed to come near them. Papa kept them away because women loosen the skins just like the way they loosen men. I learned that the batás cannot be played after sunset and that if there's thunder, you have to switch rhythms in honor of Changó.

"We all have our little manias when we play the batá. Some men open and close their mouth, other moan, whisper or move their eyes like madmen. No batá player dances, but when I play, it feels like every muscle of my body is accompanying the rhythm of the drums. I move inside so much that my bones hurt me later as if I were making physical exercises.

"There are the iyá players, who are ready to drop dead after a *toque de santo* or santería ceremony. But when someone calls out 'Omelé!' even the most exhausted drummer gets up and takes on a second wind, because he's been asked to revive and play good and strong.

"No one's ever called out 'omelé!' to me. When I play I feel so good, so fulfilled, so happy that my strength multiplies and I know no limits. People say that when you're a hundred years old, you carefully save what's left to you of life, but there's nothing greater in the world for me than playing my batás, so I don't skimp on energy. Sure, I'm 100 years old, but I'm still not ready to leave life, and I cling to life with my drums. My drums are the most important thing in the world to me."

DRUM FESTIVAL

PABLO Valier, the *composé* soloist of the purest improvisation of the St. Catherine of Ricciss Association, the Pompadour, of Guantánamo, better known as the Tumba Francesa, is working on a song in which the Creole language predominates.

The women of the Tumba, wearing long gowns amd profusely colored headscarves, take to the floor with their partners, a total of 30 couples. The *premier* drum, the one with the lowest voice, plays the *masón* rhythm with two *bulá* drums, a *catá* drum and a *tambora*, a smallest drum, directed by the whistle of the woman leader.

Then the old dancers launch a gallant court dance step with a strictly tropical movement of the hips. In their right hand, they hold beribonned maracas, while the multicolor dresses weave in and out of the dance and the different voices participate in the chorus marked by the composé or soloist.

Once again the whistle is blown and the drums fall silent, after the dancers fall back to form a circle. Then, with the repeated beat of the hoarse premier drum the *yubá* rhythm begins and the best couple takes the floor.

Suddenly the premier drum challenges the dancers to match the complexity of the music. The drum and the people complete the dance in sharp competition, while the other dancers, who wish the couple luck, decorate their bodies with handkerchiefs of bright colors that also symbolize this fiesta of the Tumba Francesa.

LASTING FAME

The Tumba Francesa, which in Congo language means a noisy festivity with drums, reached Cuba at the end of the 18th century, with the French settlers and their slaves who fled the independence uprising of the Haitian blacks.

The Tumba was first danced on the esplanades of the coffee plantations opened by the French settlers in eastern Cuba. The dancers were the domestic slaves who came over with their masters, while a composé narrated in legitimate Creole the extraordinary events in their country.

Since then the Tumba francesa has been characterized by a blend of courtly dress and dance steps with aggressive African drum music. The Tumba groups, which survive today in Santiago and Guanatánamo as folklore associations, organized mutual aid societies along the lines of the lodges of other African peoples, and like the latter, they, too, gave unconditional support to Cuba's fight for independence.

Pablo Valier, son of a mambí independence fighter and nephew of General Antonio Maceo, said that in time of war, the Spanish government authorized the Tumba francesa to hold their festivals, in the belief that they were innocent. They did not suspect that after the fiesta, late at night, arms would be hidden in the drums to be taken to the Liberation Army that operated in the nearby forests. "Here in Guantánamo," he stresses with a fine baritone voice, "they'd transport the arms along the banks of the Guaso river. Whenever a member of one of the Tumba organizations expressed a desire to join the fighting, he was sent back, because they were much more useful as members of the Tumba."

The Tumbas owe their fame not only to the solemnity of their dances, with turns and steps characteristic of late 18th century French court dances, to the longevity of their members who begin to participate as children, to the high quality of the drum playing, all of which factors are alien to the pressing need felt by those first Haitian slaves to maintain their traditions on Cuban soil. They owe their fame above all to the flexible evolution of that way of presenting the urban folklore traditions of their country, with the French forms, so that their Cuban descendants are the bearers of the most outstanding events in Cuban history.

TO DIE DANCING

Virtually no member of the Pompadour Society remembers when she or he began to dance. It may well have been several centuries ago, and almost all of them speak some Creole or try their hand at French.

For all of them, the life driving force is to be found in these dances where the breath of their ancestors is to be felt. And they all say that when it comes to dying, they wish to die dancing.

Simona Herrera, 97, present this afternoon in the small open plaza of the park in Guantánamo, is the oldest of all. The youngest and best solo dancer, with his 18 years, is José Ángel Caballero. Celestino Borrero, 81, is the *catayé*, or player of the catá drum, a primitive xylophonic drum consisting of a hollowed out tree trunk played horizontally with two sticks.

Celestino, in addition to being a unique catayé, has been improvising décimas like this one for the past half century:

> *De la tumba el catá*
> *es instrumento primero,*
> *detrás le siguen los cueros*
> *que van marcando el compás.*
> *Se siente el dulce bulá,*
> *el trinar de los tambores,*
> *y de sus alrededores*
> *todos acuden en masa*
> *a ver el mayor de plaza*
> *que saca a los bailadores.*

(The catá is the first instrument, followed by the skins that mark the beat. You can hear the sweet bulá, the song of the drums and people flock from all around to see the leader of the dance, who calls out the dancers.)

Pablo Valier, the chief composé, tells of more recent events:

> *Americano, no hay remedio.*
> *Es Fidel que gobierna a Cuba.*
> *Si tan contento que 'ten,*
> *Si no se vayan pa'su pai'.*

Ey, americano, no hay remedio.
Si Fidel gobierna a Cuba.

Si no content no si content
et si non
Nu va rete lam pei pu.[1]

(American, there's no remedy, Fidel governs Cuba. If you don't like it, go home).

GOOD QUALITY TUMBA

The Tumba francesa had its high point in the final decades of the 19th century and the first of the 20th, when they celebrated their fiestas in large ballrooms decorated with banners, paper garlands and strips of cloth. Then, those associations were ruled by a King and a Queen who today have been replaced by a male president and a female president. The old posts were modeled on Spanish civil government or the religious confraternities.

I spoke of the high point, because with the death of the oldest drummers and dancers and the loss of irreplaceable catayés and composés of the quality of Valier and Celestino Borrero, there is a gradual extinction of this way of making music that began by being French and then joined with other folklore expressions to form part of Cuban culture.

The Tumba francesa of Guantánamo, together with that of Santiago, maintain their strength of collectives that have received a centuries-old legacy. There are the four drums (five in the masón dance) to which is added a tambora, the director of the plaza who guides all the dance quadrilles and the venerable male president who appears just for fiestas.

[1] The last three lines are sung in créole. "—Ed."

The Tumba Francesa, *a Cuban folklore association*

Today the composé tells of current events with an occasional mix of patois, and high quality tumba is performed, either at La Pompadour's own hall or in open spaces belonging to factories and schools.

They perform with the same calm dignity of their forebears, who helped to make the Cuban nation.

CUBA Internacional. February 1979

EPIPHANY

THE Afro-Cuban festival of Epiphany celebrated by black slaves from early in the 17th century to the second half of the 19th century, is the most remote origin of the Havana Carnival.

Black people flocked to the capital in ox carts or packed into railroad cars bringing them from distant sugar mills to join their cabildos, mutual aid societies of each African ethnic group. Because that was the only day of the year that they felt free, they danced and sang to the point of delirium, clad in the traditional dress of their countries of origin. On all the streets leading into the Plaza de Armas, where the Palace of the Captain General, today the Museum of the City, was located, they joined the frenzied festivities of the domestic slaves who lived in the city of San Cristóbal de la Habana.

The chorus or band of masked people, identified by the banners of the cabildos and the clothing of the dancers, followed the beat of the drums with no signs of fatigue. In that orgy of religious rites, ancestral songs and *aguardiente*, cane liquor, the director of the comparsas who led the way with his three-corner hat, and the elegance of the women were outstanding. There were few women who failed to wear costly jewelry and lovely sequined gowns, while the men, clad as warriors, brandished bells of different types instead of arms.

At noon, the parade of black kings, without crowns, clad in animal skins, and queens who were protected by parasols held by elegant "ladies of the court," was joined by the *diablitos*, little devils. The diablito, fantastic character of African folklore, with his colorful costume or jute adorned with colored ribbons and bells, performed acrobatic dances characterized by a rich language of gestures, because according to mythology he must not speak.

As they passed by, the comparsas held out rustic metal boxes to collect monetary donations from the onlookers gathered on the balconies and sidewalks. Opposite the Palace with its shady courtyard, grand staircases and broad galleries, the celebration became ceremonial, and the groups danced through in perfect order.

The Congos were there, and the Lucumís, with large hats decorated with peacock feathers and red percale trousers; the Ararás, with their faces scarred since childhood, wore thick rolls of vegetable fiber around their waist. They all performed for the Spanish colonial governor the best of their folklore and received in exchange half an ounce of gold.

Then the cabildos withdrew, to fill the entire city with their rejoicing over illusory freedom.

The abolition of slavery in 1886 brought an end to the Epiphany celebration in its traditional form, although black people continued to celebrate at a given time of year, with their comparsas and striking outfits which at times called to mind those of their forebears.

At carnival time, upperclass whites gathered in the salons of the exclusive societies or in famed theaters, where they had fun in their own way. Well into the 20th century, their comparsas did not go into the streets, which were regarded as the province of the lower orders.

Carnival paseos or ride-abouts already existed from the second half of the 19th century, and they consisted of the slow passage of carriages and coaches bearing elegant ladies.

Then, in 1908, the comparsas were officially banned. The ban lasted for two decades. During the dictatorship of Gerardo Machado (1915-1933) the ban was briefly lifted, only to be reimposed because of the satyrical nature of their songs. Then, they reappeared in 1937, and carnival was limited to the Prado and part of the Malecón sea drive.

At that time the best known comparsas were Las Guaracheras de Pueblo Nuevo, an all-woman group of elegant steps; Los Kokoricamos, comprised of hooded men who danced to the beat of frying pans; Los Payasos, with their colorful outfits; Las Bolleras, dressed like Lucumís, with long, full, starched gowns, embroidered headscarves and coral hoop earrings. As they danced, the women hawked their huge trays of fritters.

Of all the comparsas, the only one still existing is El Alacrán, which made its first appearance in 1908 and which today, over three quarters of a century later, continues to open the carnival parade in the capital of revolutionary Cuba.

The famous 9 o'clock cannon shot, which centuries ago, warned the Havanans that the gates of the city were being closed and which continues to be fired every night, marks the start of today's carnival parade.

El Alacrán, comprised of 45 couples and 38 musicians, opens carnival with its traditional steps that go back to the Epiphany celebration. Slowly, the dancers, many of them old persons, repeat the routines they learned as children. With half-closed eyes, they sing all along the Havana sea drive the chant that identifies them, with its roots going back to the days of slavery: "Logoro, te llama el mayoral!" (Logoro, the overseer is calling you!). The women sing in a chorus as they hold up the full skirts of their gowns, similar to those worn by the slave women who for one day a year felt like queens of a picturesque realm.

Upon the float that accompanies the comparsa is a replica of a slave barrack, where 15 young dancers portray the January 6 celebration, in a faithful rendition of the folklore representing a very Cuban way of having fun.

CUBA Internacional (Russian edition). February 1984

MASQUERADES IN SANTIAGO

MOUNTED on horses decorated with ribbons and bells, the young men of Santiago launched Masquerade Days at the beginnning of the 19th century.

After the customary dip in the river, they entered the city on San Tadeo Street. Their noisy gallop was followed by disguised merrymakers who roved around from early in the morning to take part at 2:00 in the afternoon in the horse races on Santo Tomás Street.

At seven o'clock the ladies, dressed in luxurious linen gowns, rode through the tree-lined streets on quiet, well-behaved steeds. Their rice-powdered faces bore the barest hint of a smile: decent women did not smile in public.

Masquerade days, including the days of St. John, St. Peter, St. James Apostle and St. Anne, abounded in bonfires in the streets, reciters of praise, mummers and puppeteers, along with dances and soirees, Tumbas Francesas, private parties and rival comparsas such as those from the Los Hoyos and the Tivolí sectors.

Santiago in those days was a city surrounded by green mountains and a spacious bay, a city of low houses with dipping tile roofs and woven straw fences that survived earthquakes. The luminous whitewashed faces of the houses stood out sharply against the surrounding woods.

In the spacious Plaza de Armas, site of the House of Government, the cathedral and the mansions of the Santiago aristocracy, there were many cafés. Tables covered with pure white cloths and lighted with candles or oil lamps held cups of coffee and chocolate, bottles of beer and plates of meringue, pastries and other local sweetmeats. Steaming *ajiaco*, boiled yam and savory roast pork were the stars of the typically Cuban supper. Black women, both slaves and free who specialized in the food business, waited on the diners.

At the door of the Philharmonic Society stood an announcement for the upcoming masquerade ball for pure whites only.

With six violins, a few drums, guitars and flutes, a little orchestra of blacks improved there a minuet, a French contredanse or a rigadoon.

At the private parties in the more distant parts of town, a balladeer sang the tune of the day, accompanied by the Cuban guitar, then a novelty. According to Walter Goodman, an English painter who lived in Cuba from 1864 to 1869, at carnival time, houses were left open to the flow of passers-by and it was common for servants to "storm" the opulent homes of the rich to offer their music. Everything was permitted in that context, even speaking familiarly to the masters. At times, when they thanked the well-to-do for their gifts of food and other items, the masquerades set up a makeshift stage in the drawing room so the humble servants could put on a show.

But the chief feature of those happy days was the night time revelry of the cabildos of black slaves, the origin of the comparsas. The sound of their cowbells and *bandurrias* could hardly be heard above the ruckus made by the dancers, with their cheeks burning from cane liquor. Outstanding were the Carabalís and the Congos. The latter wore customes imitating the livery of the servants of a king who moved at the center of his retinue. Then came the "amazons," exuberant women of mixed ethnic origin who wore fine cotton gowns and walked elegantly with His Majesty, four abreast, linked to each other by the ends of huge handkerchiefs, while the military band of the make-believe court accompanied the dance with drums, noise makers, maracas and a bamboo harp that astonished the onlookers.

Also impressive was the comparsa and the *bozal* blacks, recently arrived from Africa, who died their heads orange-red and covered their faces with pink paint. Then there were the mulattoes with yellow wigs and fake beards, white males painted red and black and dressed like women. Many dancers had their clothes on inside out with the seams decorated with tin and copper strips that shone like silver and gold.

It should not be forgotten that the dance, an uncontrollable passion of African peoples, the opener of religous rites and the social binder of the community, then represented a good part of their lives. Hence they endowed with magical powers the movements and chants that sent them into a state of unreality and made them forget, in their joy, their plight as captives.

During Masquerade Days, the soirees in the exclusive societies, the horse riding of the ladies and the costumed merrymakers and the private parties were the exclusive province of the whites, while the exciting and at times grotesque street comparsas were the most important thing for those black people who plunged with their music into the heart of the city.

Revolución y cultura. June 1979

HERE COMES THE COCOYÉ

*A*BRE, *que ahí viene el cocoyé* (Make way, here comes the *cocoyé*) is the "open, sesame" of all congas in Santiago. *Abre, que ahí viene el cocoyé* pulls the Santiagueros along, it plunges them into a conga that begins on Trocha Street, swells at every corner and inevitably ends up on crowded Enramada, opposite the sea.

El cocoyé is typical of the Santiago carnival, as are the Chinese bugle, the suggestive *bocús*, drums that are tuned with fire, and the legendary Carabalí Izuamá and Olugo cabildos that launch the festivities every July 26.[1]

The singing of *El cocoyé* goes back to the arrival at the end of the 18th century on Cuba's southeastern coast of fragile ships filled with French planters from Haiti. This nostalgic song of the domestic slaves who accompanied their masters fleeing the Haitian Revolution became popular with several melodic variations, while the original word, *cocuyé*, became cocoyé because that was how black people in Santiago pronounced it.

[1] In 1953, the revolutionaries who attacked Santiago's Moncada fortress on July 26 chose the date because carnival was in progress and provided a good cover for their preparations. After 1959, July 26 became a national holiday. Santiago's week-long carnival is still held the last week in July. "—T."

Sung by all the comparsas, *El cocoyé* switched its original chorus to one of biting satire or mocking warning.

Tradition has it that on the final morning of the carnival of 1836, Juan Casamitjana, director of the band of the Catalonia regiment, was relaxing on the balcony of the Venus Hotel, opposite Plaza de Marte, when he watched a comparsa directed by two famous women, María La O, from the Tivolí district and María la Luz, from Los Hoyos, passing by. The comparsa used the couplets of *El cocoyé* as its chorus. Casamitjana was the first musician who wrote down the arrangement of *El cocoyé* with sustained modifications due to popular usage. After that, other arrangements were made. Pianist and composer Luis M. Gottschalk arranged it as a *danza* and two celebrated Cuban musicians, Amadeo Roldán and Gonzalo Roig, included their arrangements in their repertoires. In all, nine composers worked on *El cocoyé*, a record for a popular piece.

At this point in its history, the chorus of *El cocoyé* may be something like this:

> *¡Ay, ay, qué risa me da*
> *ver a la bemba 'e cuero*
> *con la boca repintá!*

(It gives me a laugh to see leather lips with her painted mouth.)

> *Filomena no está aquí*
> *que se la llevó Nicot para un cuarto de a tres pesos*
> *y los muebles de cartón.*

(Filomena isn't here, Nicot took her away, to a 3 pesos room with cardboard furniture.)

Or the best known of all, even to people who visit Santiago at carnival time:

Abre, que ahí viene el cocoyé... and the *conga*, like a magician's trick, multiplies on each corner, to die facing the port.

CUBA Internacional. April 1976

CARABALÍ DANCE

Y EYA, the oldest black woman of the Carabalí cabildo, always wears her white ruffled dress that she uses for her comparsa, when the Carabalí Izuamá meets to rehearse in a colonial courtyard in Santiago.

Sitting on her high backed chair, she waits patiently for the director to wave the *maruga* or scepter and for the Drum chief (the musical director) to order the start of playing. Then she stands up, dances a few timid steps—she is one hundred and fifteen years old—and again sits down to follow with a shining look the movements of the nearest dancers. Although Yeya began to dance with her father in the 19th century, when the slaves belonging to a given ethnic group joined lodges known as cabildos, she never tires of hearing Carabalí music.

COLONIZATION: CENTURY 1ST

When the men of conqueror Diego Velázquez found themselves without a work force to put up the first settlement of the Spanish Empire on the Island of Cuba, the town of Baracoa (1512) and because the few Indians left by genocide hardly counted, they figured that the ideal solution would be to import African slaves.

In 1532 the first slaves arrived on the coast at Baracoa. With the first lot of 1,500 Africans came their rites, beliefs, and music elements which would join with European contributions to forge the new Cuban culture.

DANCE OF KINGS

The king, dressed in red with a silver crown, stands with the queen and the princess to watch ecstatically the moves of the dancers, ladies and gentlemen of the court, who turn with ribbons, tulle and swords as they bow, while Juan Medina, duke and soloist, 77, sings the opening, *Greetings to the queen*, while the dancemaster with his top hat guides the steps to the slow beat of the *fondo*, a small drum.

At the order of the director, the music stops and the drum chief signals a change of beat. Juan Medina now sings *La invasión* (The Invasion):

> *Me miras indiferente porque soy carabalí,*
> *en la Guerra del 68 yo fui mambí;*
> *en la del 95 a la Invasión también fui*
> *a pelear por esta tierra donde nací.*

(You pay no heed to me because I'm a Carabalí, / but in the 1868 War, I was a mambí, / and in the 95 War, I joined the invasion force / to fight for this land where I was born.)

And then the chorus comes in with:

> *Ya tú lo ve, camará,*
> *el negro carabalí*
> *peleó por su libertad.*

(So you see, buddy, / Carabalí black / fought for his freedom.)

At a signal, the big drum replies and the quinto drum and the *chachás* multiply the rhythm in an *obia de ataque*, the same one played by their forebears in wartime, when there was danger.

THE BARACOAS

Olimpo Nápoles, song chief of the Carabalí Olugo:

"My father, Simón Nápoles, and his six brothers, known as *the Baracoas* because they were born in that city, were the leaders of the Izuamá cabildo at the end of the 19th century.

"In the 1895 War my uncles were officers of the Liberation Army and my father was the commander of a unit that operated near here, in El Cobre, he was a top associate of the Cuban General Guillermón Moncada. You can imagine what our life was like back then, as we fled through the mountains with my mother, with the Spaniards on our tail trying to hunt down my father. We got so used to living in the woods that one time we arrived at Hill of the Cross after a hike of four leagues. When I saw the reflectors of the ships down in the bay of Santiago, I thought they were bolts of lightning, so I kept repeating *manéfica* over and over, because that was what my elders would say when there was lightning. Then, when daylight came and I could see some men in boats, I was dazed because I just couldn't understand how they could ride around the sea sitting in crates."

SLAVERY; CENTURY 4TH

With the arrival of the last contingents of slaves from areas such as the Congo, Yorubaland and the Calabar Coast, the African presence in Cuba became more numerous in the 19th century. At the same time the expansion of the sugar plantations determined the distribution of the slaves throughout the island. And, while for the slave owners it proved to be more productive when they allowed Africans of the same origin to join mutual aid societies or lodges known as cabildos, because they did not work in isolation, for the slaves themselves: the cabildo was decisive for preserving their cultural traditions in the shape of dances and songs that brought glory to their nation of origin.

OLGA FERNÁNDEZ

ARMS USED TO TRAVEL IN TONGUE TWISTERS

Olimpo notes: "My grandmother told me that when she was a slave during the Ten Years War (1868-1878), the Carabalí men from the neighboring hills hid weapons inside drums on festive nights, and then some of them would take them to the woods, with arms and medicine hidden in the big drum, called the tongue twister. If along the way there was no danger, they played *obia marcada* (slow rhythm), but if the Spaniards drew near the camp, they let the insurgents know by playing an obia de ataque.

"My grandmother said that the masters allowed Africans to hold their fiestas because they believed that the drums and the dances made the slaves forget their longing for freedom. If they only knew what those fiestas were used for! Then, when that war ended in 1878, with the Pact of Zanjón, slavery was abolished for the slaves who had fought in the insurgent ranks alongside their masters, because the top leaders in 68 were plantation owners. Then, in 1886, slavery was totally abolished. When war broke out again in 1895, the Carabalís provided the same service to the mambises, taking advantage of the carnival, and most of the men went into the mountains to fight for their freedom. After the war, we continued to be organized in cabildos and many of us formed comparsas to take part in the carnival and show the people our songs and dances. Before, the songs were biting or insulting to the Spaniards and the bad governments of that Republic (1902-1959). Carabalí Olugo was kept from participation for 50 years. It's been only recently that it's come back, and the difference between the two cabildos is that they were organized at different sugar mills. In the carnival, Olugo represents the Tivolí district of Santiago, while Izuamá represents Los Hoyos."

TOO OLD FOR STRONG RHYTHMS

Mollú Barén for Commander Simón Baracoa; for Captain Luis Baracoa, for Lieutenants Juan *Baracoíta* and Tomás Nápoles, for first sergeant José Brígido and for Fernando and José de los Santos

Carabalí Olugo comparsa *at masquerades in Santiago*

Baracoa. Mollú Barén for all the dead of the great Carabalí Izuamá cabildo.

"This is a palpable demonstration that the founders of this great cabildo were interested not only in promoting a fraternal organization for carnival participation, but that they also answered the call of their country. Now, all that needs to be done is to verify the prayers we've dedicated to the founders and to all those who have had the misfortune to fall before us."

And Porfirio Villalón, director of Carabalí Izuamá since 1937, ends his monologue and at an order of the drum chief, begins an elegant rhythm. The couples dance and chant the final prayer:

> *Ero mi tambó,*
> *ero mi cha-chá,*
> *carabalí ya se acabó,*
> *carabalí no vuelve má.*

179

(I'm my drum, / I'm my cha-chá, / Carabalí all gone, / Carabalí won't come back.)

Says Porfirio: "Since the Revolution, I've gotten a bit more polished. I used to direct the comparsa, but now I direct a folklore company which, besides heading the carnival, performs in all the theaters of Cuba. Although we continue to sing of our love for our country and the rebelliousness of our slave forebears, today's beat is slower, because the Carabalís have gone beyond the noisy comparsa. Now the rhythm is more in tune with the new songs and our own age. We're pretty old for strong rhythms.

"As you've seen, this is a small court where the king, the queen and the princess are the only ones who don't dance, while the gentlemen get to be dukes and counts because of their dancing ability. We also use a sword for the nobles, to defend the sovereign. The people who created these dances, the Carabalí slaves, imitated the dress and the dancers of their masters, maybe to make fun of them or to get them to look more kindly upon their festivities on Masquerade Day, the day they felt like real Carabalís."

CUBA Internacional. May 1973

Afro-Cuban Terms and Spanish Words More Frequently Used in This Book

ABAKUÁ: *Secret society of Nigerian origin whose complex ritual is accompanied by spectacular music and dance.*

AJIACO: *A favorite, traditional Cuban stew made of pork, jerked beef, fresh beef, yucca, yam, sweet potato, plantain, squash, corn.*

BAMBUCO: *Colombian popular dances.*

BANDURRIA: *String instrument similar to the guitar, but smaller.*

BONGÓ: *Two small drums joined by a piece of wood, it is held on the lap to play. Played with the fingers and palms.*

BOZAL: *Blacks who did not speak Spanish well.*

CARABALÍ CABILDO: *Fraternal Institution of the slaves of Nigerian origin.*

CATIBÍA: *Yucca flour used to make a cake known as matahambre (hunger-killer).*

CENCERRO: *Cowbell, used as an instrument in the Cuban music.*

CENTÉN: *Spanish gold coin worth 100 reales.*

CHA-CHA-CHA: *Song and dance genre based on the danzón, specifically the "new beat" danzón, heavily influenced by the* son. *The cha-cha-chá was created by Enrique Jorrín at the end of the 40's. There is notable influence of the Madrid chotís.*

CÍRCULOS SOCIALES: *Recreation centers which before the Revolution were private clubs for the rich, such as the Miramar Yacht Club or the Vedado Tennis Club. They now hold weekend dances with top orchestras.*

CIRUELÓN: *Beverage made with plums and cane liquor.*

CLARINA: *Leading female singers.*

CLAVE: *Musical instrument consisting of two round sticks about 20 cm long made of hard, sonorous wood that are clicked together to keep the beat. They are used in different Cuban musical groups.*

COLUMBIA: *Variation of the rumba.*

COMPARSA: *Group of street dancers who move to the rhythm of a conga in carnival.*

CONGA: *Musical group in carnival comparsas. Its origin goes back centuries to the festivities of the black slaves in Cuba. Its members carry drums of different sizes and types, cowbells, pans and metal instruments.*

CONGRÍ: *Mixture of rice and kidney beans, very popular in Cuba.*

CONJUNTO: *Type of musical group that appeared around 1940, as a result of the enlargement of the septet. Plays* bolero, son *and* guaracha. *Generally includes piano, bass, bongo, conga drum, guitar, four trumpets and three singers. Son conjuntos have the three string guitar as their basic instrument.*

CRIOLLA (CUBAN SONG): *A vocal genre created by Luis Casas Romero. Although the lyrics often refer to rural themes, its genesis and development are urban.*

CRIOLLO (A) (CREOLE): *In the Americas, a person born in the region, or anything that is characteristic of it. It also refers to the native condition.*

DANZONIZACION: *To set Cuban songs in* danzón *rhythm.*

DÉCIMAS: *Metric combination of 10 octosyllabic verses. Very much used in Cuban country music.*

ENKANIKÁ: *A sort of little cowbell.*

FEELING: *From the English word. Genre within the Cuban song that arose in the 40's as a need for transformation. Notable influence of United States music. The feeling movement included composers, singers and arrangers.*

GUAGUANCÓ: *A type of rumba.*

GUAJIRA: *A song similar to the criolla with lyrics on rural matters approached in a buccolic, idyllic fashion. It usually uses the décima model.*

GUAJIRO: *In Cuba, a rural person or farmer.*

GUAYABERA: *A loose, pleated shirt with pockets whose use has become generalized in Cuba and other Latin American countries.*

GUAYO: *See güiro.*

GÜIRO: *Common musical instrument, probably of Bantú origin. It is also known as guayo and is made of a gourd from 30 to 50 cm long, with a curved projection. Its front surface has several parallel grooves that cross the güiro axis, so that when they are rubbed with a hard stick, a musical sound is made.*

HABANERA: *Its origin goes back to the Creole dance. Very popular in the second half of the 19th century. Its structural elements appear in pieces by European composers such as Albéniz, Ravel, Debussy. It also influenced the Argentine tango.*

ILÉ: *In Yoruba language means lodge.*

JUTIA: *A cat-size rodent that abounds in the Antilles. Its meat is regarded as a delicacy.*

KIMBILA: *A sort of African danza, similar to a little xylophone.*

LENIN PARK: *Unique in Latin America for its size and the wide variety of its facilities. Located southwest of Havana on 745 ha. Has restaurants, art galleries, open air cinema, amusement park, rodeo stadium, aquarium and a natural amphitheater with the stage in a lake.*

MAMBÍ (SES): *Cuban insurgents who fought Spanish colonial rule.*

MARACAS: *Typical of, but not native to, Cuba. Consists of a closed receptacle made of a gourd, or of wood, with seeds inside that make a sound when the maracas is shaken.*

MARIMBULA: *Instrument used by son groups. Its origin is believed to be the African sansa or mbila. It is also used in other Caribbean countries. It consists of a wooden box with steel strips fastened in the center. When the ends of the strips are fingered, they produce vibrations in the box. It is used as a stand-in for the bass.*

MARUGA: *An Afro-Cuban rattle made of two empty metal cones soldered at the base. The surface of the cones is perforated and the ends are cut off, with a handle at one end.*

MONTUNO: *Rhythmic chorus of a son.*

PUNTO GUAJIRO: *Rural song with Andalusian roots. Since the 17th century African influence is to be noted. Accompanied by guitars, tres, tiple, lute, claves and güiro. The singers improvise on different themes. There are two styles, the* punto fijo, *in which the singer follows a single melody, and the* punto libre, *in which the melody is more flexible.*

SIBONEÍSMO: *The cult of people and traditions of the pre-Columbian period.*

SOLAR: *Tenement of one-room units built around a courtyard that served as a community social space.*

SONERO MAYOR: *Name given to the best and most beloved singers of the* son.

SUCU-SUCU: *Onomatopoeic name given to the dance, music and family parties where it is played.*

TABURETE: *Rustic seat used by Cuban farmers.*

TIMBALES: *Brass cymbals.*

TRES: *Three stringed guitar, typical of Cuba, mainly used in son and punto guajiro.*

TROVA MAYOR: *The most important singers and composers of the traditional Cuban song.*

TROVADOR(ES): *Singers and musicians who entertain in serenades and parties.*

VIHUELA: *An ancient type of guitar.*

ZAPATEO CUBANO: *Country dance, descendent of the Andalusian zapateo and related to similar Latin America dances. Based on the same principles of the* punto guajiro. *Consists of tapping constantly with the heels to mark the beat. The zapateo was reported to exist early in the 18th century. Its high point came in the second half of the 19th century although it continued to be quite popular in the first decades of the 20th. Today, it has practically disappeared.*

ZAPATEADO: *Stamping with heel and toe.*

Appendix[*]

ACOSTA LEON, ANGEL (1932-64),
painter, graduated from San Alejandro Art Academy in Havana,
and received national awards and a prize in the Second Inter American Biennial in Mexico; some of his most important paintings in
the National Museum of Fine Arts in Havana are Coffeemaker No.
1, Peace Carrousel and Anvil.

ADAMS, SALVADOR (1894-1971),
guitarist and composer; author of of important popular songs,
such as Altiva es la palma (Proud is the palmtree) and Mi sublime
obsesión (My sublime obsession).

ALMENARES, ANGEL (1902-),
guitarist and composer; studied music at the Academy of Fine
Arts of Cuba; author of boleros, among them Ya te olvidé (I have
already forgotten you).

[*] When the personality's nationality is not especified, it is because they are
Cubans. Those of international fame are not included. The main bibliography
consulted for this Appendix was the Diccionario de la música cubana. Biográ-
fico y técnico, by Helio Orovio, Ed. Letras Cubanas, 1981. —Ed.

BALLAGAS, PATRICIO (1879-1920),
composer and guitarist; composed his songs in 4x4, known as
compasillo, *but his major contribution was the use of the double*
text and the melody superimposed on the song of the second voice
in two apart harmony.

BANDERAS, JOSE (1891-1967),
composer and guitarist; professor of guitarist Vicente González
Rubiera (Guyún).

BARROSO, ABELARDO (1905-72),
singer, member of the Havana Sextet first, and later on of son
groups and "typical orchestras" as a performer of danzonete.

BLEZ, EMILIANO (1879-1973),
composer, guitarist and troubadour; author of boleros.

BAMBU, IGNACIO (1914-73),
guitarist and composer of Amargas penas *(Bitter pain) and the popular*
Cuatro pollos, cinco reales *(Four chickens, five cents), among others.*

CAIGNET, FELIX B. (1892-1976),
composer of Frutas de El Caney *(Fruits of El Caney), which gained*
great popularity and is still played; also the author of radio soap
operas.

CASAMITJANA, JUAN (Barcelona, 1805-1882),
flautist, composer, teacher and conductor; included forms of local
musical folklore in his pieces.

CORONA, MANUEL (1880-1950),
composer and guitarist, one of the greatest of Cuban troubadours;
author of guarachas inspired *by current events.*

CUETO, RAFAEL (1900-91), *guitarist and singer, created a rhythmic model* (tumbao) *based on a melodic rhythmic movement with the bases to which percussion is added; it is outstanding because of its Cuban flavor.*

CUNI, MIGUELITO (1920-84), *singer and composer, sang with the most important Cuban orchestras, such as Arcaño y sus maravillas (Arcaño and His Marvels), Arsenio Rodríguez's group, Benny Moré's Giant Band, and Chapottín Orchestra.*

CHAPPOTIN, FELIX (1909-83), *trumpeter, director of the orchestra that bears his name; belonged to the Havana Sextet; in the 50's he joined Arsenio Rodríguez's orchestra, which subsequently took his name when he became the conductor.*

DELFIN, EUSEBIO (1893-1965), *composer, guitarist and singer, thought up the typical twang of* bolero *accompaniment used in the 20's to an original semi-arpeggio rhythm.*

DELGADO, MANUEL (1876-1925), *guitarist and composer, his songs include* La Gacela *(The Gazelle),* Aquel beso robado *(That stolen kiss), among others.*

DIEZ, BARBARITO (b. 1909), *singer, in 1935 joined the Antonio María Romeu orchestra where he stayed ever since; now the orchestra bears his named.*

EMBALE, CARLOS (b. 1923), *singer of sones and* guarachas, *was member of the Boloña and Bolero septets, and the Matamoros group; in 1976 started to sing* with the National Septet; now directs a guaguancó group that bears his name.

ESTUDIANTINA ORIENTAL, group organized in Santiago in eastern Cuba at the end of the 19th century; played boleros, sones, guarachas and was made up of a three-string guitar, marímbula, cymbals, Cuban kettle drum, maracas, claves, guitar and two singers; first orchestral organizations that played the Cuban son in the first and second decades of the 20th century.

ICAIC SOUND EXPERIMENTATION, group founded in 1970 under the sponsorship of the Cuban Film Institute, under the direction of Leo Brouwer; has developed an experimental line in Cuban and Latin American music, creatively transforming folklore contributions.

FAILDE, MIGUEL (1852-1921), composer, cornet player and orchestra director, creator of the danzón; also played the viola and bass and played in a number of concerts of classical music; in 1871 he founded his typical orchestra.

FEIJOO, SAMUEL (1914-92), folklorist, poet and writer, did outstanding work in folklore research and compilation; promoter of Cuban popular art; the magazines Islas and Signos, which he edited, published his works.

FERNANDEZ, TERESITA (b. 1930), singer, guitarist and composer, her songs are a mixture of poetry and music and center on nature, daily life; composer of children's songs such as Tía Jutía (Aunt Jutia), Canta, pajarito (Sing, Little Bird) and others of intimate lyricism.

FIGAROLA, JOSE (1893-19?),

composer and singer of ballads, disciple of Sindo Garay, also learned from Pepe Sánchez and Emilano Blez, the great Cuban troubadors; directed the Trio Oriental.

FORNARIS, JOSE (1827-90),

poet, a graduate attorney, he took part in independent struggles; in literature was identified with the "Nativist" current. The most outstanding author of the "Siboneyist" current, with his Cantos del Siboney (Songs of the Siboney Indian).

GARAY, SINDO (1867-1968),

composer, singer guitarist, highest exponent of the troubadour ballads in Cuba. Self-taught, he possessed extraordinary intuition. Transformed the style of the Cuban ballads by introducing new sounds. The lyrics of his songs are very poetical.

GOMEZ, RAFAEL (1889-1971),

composer, known in the musical world as Teofilito. Played guitar, flute, clarinet, bass, accordion and cymbals.

GONZALEZ RUBIERA, VICENTE (1908-87),

guitarist and teacher of harmony, known as Guyún. He began his guitar studies with Pepe Banderas and Sindo Garay, in the 30's he was the best troubadour in his vocal interpretations and instrumentals, of Cuban music and that of Latin American countries He and his many pupils founded a Cuban guitar school. He wrote The guitar, its technique using the pinky finger of the right hand and the thumb of the left to achieve more complete harmonies. In his guitar transcriptions he used a new system of annotation.

HAVANA SEXTET,

founded in 1920 in Havana, its predecessor was the Orient Quartet which became a sextet and changed its name to "Habanero". In 1927 the group became a Septet.

IBAÑEZ, JOSE (1875-1987), *tres player, singer and composer, known as* Chicho, *had an original style of singing sones and songs of Abakuá origin.*

INCIARTE, RAFAEL (1909-91), *composer, band director, saxophonist and clarinetist, author of studies on autochthonous music, especially of eastern Cuba; belonged to symphony orchestras and to dance orchestra.*

IRAKERE, *musical group founded in 1973; its members include some of Cuba's best musicians and from the start, it has held a top place in Cuban popular music; its line takes off from the basic elements of Cuban folklore, traditional dance music and universal sound forms, incorporating the possibilities of electronic music and current expressive tendencies. The director is Jesús* (Chucho) *Valdés.*

LASALLE, ANA (b. Paris, 1919), *actress and director, has lived in Cuba since 1957 and works for radio and TV; has won a number of national awards.*

LECUONA, ERNESTINA (1882-1951), *pianist and composer, sister of composer Ernesto Lecuona; as a pianist she gave concerts in Cuba and America; author of* Anhelo besarte *(I Long to Kiss You),* Ya que te vas *(Since You're Going Away).*

LECUONA, ERNESTO (1896-1963), *composer and pianist; came to be one of the best known composers; a gifted pianist of exceptional qualities, he made contributions to the Cuban piano art especially in the use of certain rhythms; He wrote over 600 pieces including the well-known* Siempre en mi corazón *(Always in My Heart) and* Malagueña.

191

LEON, ARGELIERS (1918-91),
musicologist, composer, teacher; directed (1961-1970) the Institute of Ethnology and Folklore of the Academy of Sciences of Cuba; taught at the Havana Municipal Conservatory and Havana University, where he was professor of African art and Black cultures of Cuba; his compositions are based chiefly on folklore music, but using sophisticated technical elements.

MACEO GRAJALES, ANTONIO (1845-96),
Cuban patriot, fought as 1st colonel in Cuba's war of independence from Spanish colonial rule; fell in battle, in an apotheosis of glory and bravery.

MARINELLO, JUAN (1898-1977),
lawyer and writer, studied law at Havana University; wrote for Cuban magazines and for the most important publications in Latin America; served as Cuban ambassador to UNESCO and member of the Central Committee of the Communist Party of Cuba; his vast literary work has been translated into a number of languages.

MARQUETTI, JOSE (1909-67),
singer, known as Cheo, he was outstanding during the danzonete fad, which he sang with popular Cuban orchestras, in the 30's; he cultivated the guajira-son and attained popularity.

MARQUEZ, RAMON (1908-80),
ballader, as a second voice in harmony, he sang with duets and trios in his home town.

MARTINEZ FURE, ROGELIO (b. 1927),
folklorist, worked at the Institute of Ethnology and Folklore of the Academy of Sciences of Cuba, specializing in the study and dissemination of African cultural influence in America; in 1962 he founded the National Folklore Company, and with it, toured

countries in Europe and Africa; has published many articles in Cuban and foreign magazines, along with the book Imaginary Dialogues and a two-volume anthology of African poetry, among others; also the author of musical pieces.

MARTINEZ, VILLENA (1899-1934), lawyer, poet, and political fighter, joined the Communist Party in 1927 and later became a member of its central committee.

MELLA, JULIO ANTONIO (1903-29), revolutionary leader and intellectual, played an active role in the struggle against the Machado dictatorship (1929-34); founded the Communist Party in 1925; wrote articles in magazines and in the revolutionary press of Cuba and Mexico; was assassinated in Mexico City in 1929 by Machado agents.

MORE, BENNY, (1919-63), composer and singer, one of the most brilliant figure, of Cuban popular music; shone in all the Cuban genres; sang with the orchestra of Dámaso Pérez Prado and the Matamoros, and in 1953 founded his own orchestra, creating an original style that made him extremely popular.

NATIONAL FOLKLORE COMPANY, founded on May 7, 1962 in Havana under the direction of Rogelio Martínez Furé and Mexican Rodolfo Reyes Cortés. It has compiled and staged Cuban dance and musical expressions on the basis of folklore research. The company has received a number of awards and has conducted international tours.

NICOLA, ISAAC (b. 1916), guitarist and teacher of guitar, played concerts and gave lectures in different countries; in 1951 became a teacher and later the director of the Havana Municipal Conservatory; headed the Scientific-technical Council for Music Education.

ORTIZ, FERNANDO (1881-1969),

ethnographer, lawyer, archeologist, linguist and historian, was a professor at the University of Havana; for many years he served as president of the Economic Association of Friends of the Country; founded the Cuban Folklore Association in 1923, the Hispano-Cuban Culture Institute in 1926 and the Association of the Afro-Cuban Studies in 1937; also founded important magazines; was nominated for a Nobel Peace Prize; for several years he headed the National Board of Archeology and Ethnography of Cuba.

ORTIZ, RAFAEL (b. 1908),

guitarist and composer, has directed the Ignacio Piñeiro Septet for many years; author of the bolero-son, guarachas *and songs.*

PIÑEIRO, IGNACIO (1888-1969),

composer, self taught, worked in a number of groupe beginning in 1903; in 1928 founded the National Sextet which later became a septet; George Gershwin met him in Havana and was inspired by his son-pregon Echale salsita *(Put sauce on it) for his* Cuban Overture; *Piñeiro composed* guaguancos, danzones, sones, tango congos.

PONCE, FIDELIO (1895-1949),

painter, studied for a few years at San Alejandro Academy of Fine Arts; won prizes in National salons; his paintings Las beatas *(Churchgoers) and* Paisaje *(Landscape), among others, can be seen at Cuba's Museum of Fine Arts.*

PORTELA, PAQUITO (1889-1975),

composer and guitarist, played the bass and belonged to several popular music groups.

POVEDA, FRANCISCO (1796-1881),

poet, known by the name of El Trovador cubano; *considered as the beginer of* criollismo *in Cuban poetry;* La guirnalda habanera *(Havana Garland) is one of his books of poetry.*

PRATS, JORGE LUIS (b. 1956), *pianist, graduate in 1978 of the National School of Art, in 1977 he won the First Grand prize in the Marguerite Long-Jacques Thibaud contest in Paris, in which he also won the award as the best performer and the Ravel Prize, receiving the praise of critics and the public; in 1970 he won the gold medal in the Katia Popa Laureates Festival in Pleven, Bulgaria.*

PRATS, RODRIGO (1909-80), *composer, violinist, pianist and orchestra director, was founder-conductor of the Simphony Orchestra of the Air, the Chamber Orchestra of the Fine Arts Association, assistant director of the Havana Philharmonic, founder-director of the Jorge Anckermann Theater Company; author of songs and important zarzuelas (operettas).*

REVUELTA, RAQUEL (b. 1925), *actress in theater, radio and TV, began her career in 1941 and the following year worked with the Eugenia Zuffoli company; in 1943-44 worked in Popular theater, of which is a founding member; also worked as an actress on Cuba's Radio 1010, in the Our Time Association, the Radio Union and channel 4 TV; founder of Studio Theater.*

RIVERA, NIÑO (b. 1919), *tres player and composer, his real name is Andrés Hechevarría; began with the Caridad Sextet; in 1954 formed his own group; has been outstanding for his instrumental work; author of songs, cha-cha-chás and sones.*

RODRIGUEZ, ARSENIO (1911-72), *composer and tres player, in the 30' joined the Havana son performers; in 1940 he founded his own group, which became very popular; is known as "the marvelous blind man" because he lost his sight at the age of 13; author of sones and boleros.*

RODRIGUEZ, EZEQUIEL (b. 1913), musicologist, in 1962 headed the popular music section of the Havana office of the National Council of Culture; has published articles on Cuban composers and music; also directed Havana's House of the Troubadours.

ROIG, GONZALO (1890-1970), composer and orchestra director, regarded as the pioneer of symphonic music in Cuba; in 1929 founded the Ignacio Cervantes Orchestra and in 1938, the National Opera; author of Cecilia Valdés, regarded as the most representative work of the Cuban zarzuela or operetta.

ROLDAN, AMADEO (Paris, 1900-39), composer, violinist, teacher and conductor; with Alejandro García Caturla launched modern Cuban symphonic music; composed his Overture on Cuban themes, using elements of musical folklore; in 1926, with Alejo Carpentier, organized the concerts of New Music; founded the National School of Music of Havana; today the Conservatory of Havana bears his name.

RUBALCAVA, MANUEL JUSTO DE (1769-1805), poet and soldier, was a skilled writer of sonnets on the bucolic theme; in 1848 his verses appeared in the book Poesía de don Manuel Justo de Rubalcava.

RUIZ, ROSENDO (1885-), composer and teacher, directed the Cuban Quartet and in 1934, the Blue Trio; author of sones, songs, and guarachas.

SALAS, ESTEBAN (1725-1803), composer of church music, taught plainsong, philosophy and moral theology at the San Basilio Seminar; his music belongs to the new style of the end of the baroque period, with notable elements of classicism.

SANCHEZ, JOSE (1856-1918),

composer and guitar player, produced admirable works although he knew nothing about musical technique; one of the greatest of Cuban troubadours.

VALDES, CHUCHO (b. 1941),

pianist, composer and arranger, in the 60's organized a group with which he made innovations in Cuban music; as a member of Cuban Modern Music Orchestra, founded the Irakere group; regarded by international critics as one of the world's four best jazz pianists; his main contribution is in his original arrangements of popular pieces.

VALENZUELA, RAIMUNDO (1848-1905),

orchestra director, arranger, trombonist, composed contradances, guarachas and mainly danzones, in addition to some classical, chamber and religious works. Wrote zarzuelas (opperettas) and arranged as danzones arias of such Italian operas as Rigoletto, Tosca.

VERA, MARIA TERESA (1895-1965),

singer, guitarist and composer, an important exponent of Cuban music; for 25 years sang with trobadour Lorenzo Hierrezuelo; her compositions are still played.

VILLALON, ALBERTO (1882-1955),

composer, guitarist, troubadour, one of the greats of the traditional trova; taught guitar and recorded a number of Cuban songs; founded the National Sextet with Ignacio Piñeiro and Juan de la Cruz in 1927; composed fine songs and boleros such as La palma *(The Palmtree),* Yo reiré cuando tú llores *(I'll laugh when you cry).*

VITIER, CINTIO (b. 1921),

poet, writer, now works as researcher at the Martí Studies Institute; his books include Lo cubano en la poesía *(The Cuban Aspect in Poetry),* Los poetas románticos cubanos *(The Cuban Romantic Poets), among other volumes.*

URFE, ODILIO (1921-88), *musicologist, pianist, teacher and dance orchestra conductor, in 1931 founded the Institute of Folklore Research with the cooperation of other outstanding figures of Cuban culture of the time; directed the seminar for research into Cuban music, which now bears his name.*

WHITE, JOSE (1836-1918), *composer, violinist, teacher, knew how to play 16 instruments; gained renown as violinist in Paris and Cuba; accused of involvement in Cuban independence activities, had to escape to Mexico; later on in Venezuela founded the Classical Concert Society; his outstanding works include* Cuarteto, Seis estudios brillantes *(Six Brilliant Studies, for violin) and his universally known* La bella cubana *(The beautiful Cuban woman).*

OLGA FERNÁNDEZ
(Santa Clara, Cuba, 1943)

SHE has worked as a journalist in *CUBA Internacional* magazine for about ten years. A winner of two prizes (1980, 1986) on historical narration, and one prize (1983) on short story within La Edad de Oro literary contest, she was also awarded with mentions (1980, 1981, 1982) on child and youth literature, including one first mention (1984) in Cuba Writers and Artists Association (UNEAC) literary contest. Her works in reportage, article and interview genres have received awards in the University of Havana 13 de Marzo Contest.

Olga Fernández's books include: *Los frutos de un mañana* (Tomorrow's Harvest), 1980; *Por esta independencia* (For This Independence), 1982; *Cuba a simple vista* (Cuba at a First Glance), 1983; *En do mayor* (In C major), 1984; *Dos días con el General Antonio* (Two Days with General Antonio), 1984; *Con mi abuelo y sus amigos* (Along with my grandfather and his friends), 1986; *A pura guitarra y tambor*, 1985; *Instantes de una historia* (Moments of a History) and *La mujer y el sentido del humor* (Woman and the Sense of Humor), an anthology of humoristic short stories written by the most outstanding female Cuban authors.